INTO THE WOODS

INTO THE WOODS

Music & Lyrics by STEPHEN SONDHEIM

Book by JAMES LAPINE

THEATRE COMMUNICATIONS GROUP
NEW YORK

Into the Woods is published by Theatre Communications Group, Inc.,
520 Eighth Avenue, 24th Floor, New York, NY 10018-4156.

This publication is made possible in part by the New York State Council on the Arts with the support of Governor Andrew Cuomo and the New York State Legislature.

TCG books are exclusively distributed to the book trade by Consortium Book Sales and Distribution.

A catalogue record for this book is available from the Library of Congress.

ISBN 978-1-55936-499-7 (paperback)
ISBN 978-1-55936-816-2 (ebook)

Cover art and photographs: Copyright © 2014 Disney Enterprises, Inc.

Insert: Photographs by Peter Mountain

First Edition, May 1989
New Edition, November 2014

For Phoebe Lapine

INTO THE WOODS

ABOUT THE PLAY

Into the Woods was produced on Broadway by Heidi Landesman, Rocco Landesman, Rick Steiner, M. Anthony Fisher, Frederic H. Mayerson and Jujamcyn Theaters at the Martin Beck Theatre on November 5, 1987. It was directed by James Lapine. Scenic design was by Tony Straiges, lighting design was by Richard Nelson, costume design was by Ann Hould-Ward and sound design was by Alan Stieb and James Brousseau. The orchestrations were by Jonathan Tunick and musical direction was by Paul Gemignani. The cast was:

Narrator, Mysterious Man	Tom Aldredge
Cinderella	Kim Crosby
Jack	Ben Wright
Baker	Chip Zien
Baker's Wife	Joanna Gleason
Cinderella's Stepmother	Joy Franz
Florinda	Kay McClelland
Lucinda	Lauren Mitchell
Jack's Mother	Barbara Bryne
Little Red Ridinghood	Danielle Ferland
Witch	Bernadette Peters
Cinderella's Father	Edmund Lyndeck
Cinderella's Mother, Grandmother, Giant	Merle Louise
Wolf, Cinderella's Prince	Robert Westenberg
Rapunzel	Pamela Winslow
Rapunzel's Prince	Chuck Wagner
Steward	Philip Hoffman
Snow White	Jean Kelly
Sleeping Beauty	Maureen Davis

Into the Woods was originally workshopped at Playwrights Horizons in New York City, and first produced at the Old Globe Theatre in San Diego, California, in December 1986.

CHARACTERS

NARRATOR

CINDERELLA

JACK

JACK'S MOTHER

BAKER

BAKER'S WIFE

CINDERELLA'S STEPMOTHER

FLORINDA

LUCINDA

CINDERELLA'S FATHER

LITTLE RED RIDINGHOOD

WITCH

CINDERELLA'S MOTHER

MYSTERIOUS MAN

WOLF

GRANNY

RAPUNZEL

RAPUNZEL'S PRINCE

CINDERELLA'S PRINCE

STEWARD

GIANT

SNOW WHITE

SLEEPING BEAUTY

MUSICAL NUMBERS

ACT ONE

PROLOGUE: INTO THE WOODS. . . . . .Company
HELLO, LITTLE GIRL . . . . .Wolf, Little Red Ridinghood
I GUESS THIS IS GOODBYE . . . . .Jack
MAYBE THEY'RE MAGIC . . . . .Baker's Wife
I KNOW THINGS NOW. . . . . .Little Red Ridinghood
A VERY NICE PRINCE . . . . .Cinderella, Baker's Wife
GIANTS IN THE SKY. . . . . .Jack
AGONY . . . . .Cinderella's Prince, Rapunzel's Prince
IT TAKES TWO . . . . .Baker, Baker's Wife
STAY WITH ME . . . . .Witch
ON THE STEPS OF THE PALACE . . . . .Cinderella
EVER AFTER . . . . .Narrator, Company

ACT TWO

PROLOGUE: SO HAPPY . . . . .Company
AGONY . . . . .Cinderella's Prince, Rapunzel's Prince
LAMENT . . . . .Witch
ANY MOMENT . . . . .Cinderella's Prince, Baker's Wife
MOMENTS IN THE WOODS . . . . .Baker's Wife
YOUR FAULT . . . . .Jack, Baker, Witch,
                           Cinderella, Little Red Ridinghood
LAST MIDNIGHT . . . . .Witch
NO MORE. .Baker, Mysterious Man
NO ONE IS ALONE. . . . . .Cinderella,
                           Little Red Ridinghood, Baker, Jack
FINALE: CHILDREN WILL LISTEN . . . . . . .Witch, Company

ACT ONE

Scene 1

Downstage, three structures:
Far left, the home of Cinderella. She is in the
kitchen, cleaning.
Center, the cottage where Jack lives. He is inside,
milking his pathetic-looking cow, Milky-White.
Far right, the home/workplace of the Baker and his
Wife. They are preparing tomorrow's bread.
Behind these homes, a drop depicts a large forest
which separates them from the rest of the kingdom.
A Narrator steps forward.

NARRATOR: Once upon a time—

Music, sharp and steady. Light on Cinderella.

CINDERELLLA (*Singing to us*):
　　I wish . . .

NARRATOR: —in a far-off kingdom—
CINDERELLA:
　　More than anything . . .

NARRATOR: —lived a young maiden—
CINDERELLA:
　　More than life . . .

NARRATOR: —a sad young lad—

Light on Jack and the cow.

CINDERELLA:
　　More than jewels . . .

JACK (*To us*):
　　I wish . . .

NARRATOR: —and a childless baker—

Light on the Baker and his Wife.

3

JACK:

> More than life . . .

CINDERELLA, BAKER:

> I wish . . .

NARRATOR: —with his wife.

JACK:

> More than anything . . .

CINDERELLA, BAKER, JACK:

> More than the moon . . .

WIFE:

> I wish . . .

CINDERELLA:

> The King is giving a Festival.

BAKER, WIFE:

> More than life . . .

JACK:

> I wish . . .

CINDERELLA:

> I wish to go to the Festival—

BAKER, WIFE:

> More than riches . . .

CINDERELLA:

> —and the Ball . . .

JACK:

> I wish my cow would give us some milk.

CINDERELLA, WIFE:

> More than anything . . .

BAKER:

> I wish we had a child.

JACK (*To cow*):

> Please, pal—

WIFE:

> I want a child . . .

JACK:
> Squeeze, pal . . .

CINDERELLA:
> I wish to go to the Festival.

JACK (*Overlapping*):
> I wish you'd give us some milk
> Or even cheese . . .

BAKER, WIFE (*Overlapping*):
> I wish we might have a child.

ALL FOUR:
> I wish . . .

> *Cinderella's Stepmother and stepsisters, Florinda and Lucinda, enter.*

STEPMOTHER (*To Cinderella*):
> *You* wish to go to the Festival?

NARRATOR: The poor girl's mother had died—
STEPMOTHER:
> You, Cinderella, the Festival?
> *You* wish to go to the Festival?

FLORINDA (*Overlapping*):
> What, *you*, Cinderella, the Festival?
> The Festival?!

LUCINDA (*Overlapping*):
> What, *you* wish to go to the Festival?!

ALL THREE:
> The Festival?!
> The King's Festival!!!???

NARRATOR: —and her father had taken for his new wife—
STEPMOTHER:
> The *Festival*!!!???

NARRATOR: —a woman with two daughters of her own.
FLORINDA (*To Cinderella*):
> Look at your nails!

LUCINDA:
> Look at your dress!

STEPMOTHER:
> People would laugh at you—

CINDERELLA:
> Nevertheless—

CINDERELLA:	STEPSISTERS:	STEPMOTHER:
I still wish to go	You still wish to go	She still wants to go
To the Festival.	To the Festival—	To the Festival—

STEPSISTERS, STEPMOTHER:
> —and dance before the Prince?!

> *They chortle with laughter musically, then fall about out of control. Music stops.*

NARRATOR: All three were beautiful of face, but vile and black of heart.

> *Music resumes.*

> Jack, on the other hand, had no father, and his mother—

JACK'S MOTHER (*Entering*):
> I wish . . .

NARRATOR: Well, she was not quite beautiful—

JACK'S MOTHER:
> I wish my son were not a fool.
> I wish my house was not a mess.
> I wish the cow was full of milk.
> I wish the walls were full of gold—
> I wish a lot of things . . .

> (*To Jack, music continuing under*) You *foolish* child! What in heaven's name are you doing with the cow inside the house?

JACK: A warm environment might be just what Milky-White needs to produce his milk.

JACK'S MOTHER (*Beat; flabbergasted*): It's a she! How many times must I tell you? Only "she"'s can give milk.

> *Two knocks on the Baker's door; Wife opens door; it is Little Red Ridinghood.*

WIFE: Why, come in, little girl.

6

LITTLE RED RIDINGHOOD:
>I wish . . .
>
>It's not for me,
>It's for my granny in the woods.
>A loaf of bread, please—
>To bring my poor old hungry
>Granny in the woods . . .
>>(*Insistent*)
>Just a loaf of bread, please . . .

Baker gives her a loaf of bread.

NARRATOR: Cinderella's stepmother had a surprise for her.

Stepmother throws a pot of lentils into the fire-place.

STEPMOTHER: I have emptied a pot of lentils into the ashes for you. If you have picked them out again in two hours' time, you shall go to the Ball with us.

Stepmother and stepsisters exit.

LITTLE RED RIDINGHOOD:
>And perhaps a sticky bun? . . .
>Or four? . . .
>>(*Smiles sheepishly*)

CINDERELLA:
>Birds in the sky,
>Birds in the eaves,
>In the leaves,
>In the fields,
>In the castles and ponds . . .

LITTLE RED RIDINGHOOD:
>. . . and a few of those pies . . .

CINDERELLA (*Overlapping*):
>Come, little birds,
>Down from the eaves
>And the leaves,
>Over fields,
>Out of castles and ponds . . .

7

JACK:
> No, *squeeze*, pal . . .

CINDERELLA (*Falling into a trance*):
> Ahhh . . .

> *Music continues as birds descend to the fireplace.*

> Quick, little birds,
> Flick through the ashes.
> Pick and peck, but swiftly,
> Sift through the ashes
> Into the pot . . .

> *Birds start picking at the lentils and dropping
> them into the pot, each one landing with a clang;
> music continues under.*

JACK'S MOTHER: Listen well, son. Milky-White must be taken to
market.

> *Clangs continue under as the birds work.*

JACK: But, Mother, no—he's the best cow—
JACK'S MOTHER: Was. Was! *She's* been dry for a week. We've no
food nor money and no choice but to sell her while
she can still command a price.
JACK: But Milky-White is my best friend in the whole world!
JACK'S MOTHER: Look at her!

> There are bugs on her dugs.
> There are flies in her eyes.
> There's a lump on her rump
> Big enough to be a hump—

JACK:
> But—

JACK'S MOTHER:
> Son,
> We've no time to sit and dither,
> While her withers wither with her—

> *Two clangs.*

> And no one keeps a cow for a friend!

8

Sometimes I fear you're touched.

Little Red Ridinghood has been compulsively eating sweets at the Baker's house; she now swallows, wiping her hands and mouth.

LITTLE RED RIDINGHOOD:
> Into the woods,
> It's time to go,
> I hate to leave,
> I have to, though.
> Into the woods—
> It's time, and so
> I must begin my journey.

> Into the woods
> And through the trees
> To where I am
> Expected, ma'am,
> Into the woods
> to Grandmother's house—
>   (*Mouth full*)
> Into the woods
> To Grandmother's house—

WIFE: You're certain of your way?
LITTLE RED RIDINGHOOD:
> The way is clear,
> The light is good,
> I have no fear,
> Nor no one should.
> The woods are just trees,
> The trees are just wood.
> I sort of hate to ask it,
> But do you have a basket?

BAKER: Don't stray and be late.
WIFE: And save some of those sweets for Granny!
LITTLE RED RIDINGHOOD:
> Into the woods
> And down the dell,
> The path is straight,
> I know it well.

Into the woods,
And who can tell
What's waiting on the journey?

Into the woods
To bring some bread
To Granny who
Is sick in bed.
Never can tell
What lies ahead.
For all that I know,
She's already dead.

But into the woods,
Into the woods,
Into the woods
To Grandmother's house
And home before dark!

The birds have helped Cinderella with her task and are flying off.

CINDERELLA:
Fly, birds,
Back to the sky,
Back to the eaves
And the leaves
And the fields
And the—

Florinda and Lucinda enter, dressed for the Ball.

FLORINDA:
Hurry up and do my hair, Cinderella!
(*To Lucinda, as Cinderella fusses with her hair*)
Are you really wearing *that*?

LUCINDA (*Pointing to her sleeve*):
Here, I found a little tear, Cinderella!
(*To Florinda, eyeing her hair*)
Can't you hide it with a hat?

CINDERELLA:
You look beautiful.

FLORINDA:
 I know.

LUCINDA:
 She means me.

FLORINDA (*To Cinderella*):
 Put it in a twist.

LUCINDA:
 Who will be there? . . .

 She and Florinda continue babbling underneath.

CINDERELLA (*To herself*):
 Mother said be good,
 Father said be nice,
 That was always their advice.
 So be nice, Cinderella,
 Good, Cinderella,
 Nice good good nice—

FLORINDA:
 Tighter!

CINDERELLA:
 What's the good of being good
 If everyone is blind
 Always leaving you behind?
 Never mind, Cinderella,
 Kind Cinderella—
  (*Accenting each word with a twist of a strand of hair*)
 Nice good nice kind good nice—

FLORINDA (*Screams and slaps Cinderella*):
 Not *that* tight!

CINDERELLA (*Backing away*): Sorry.
FLORINDA: Clod.

 A beat.

LUCINDA:
 Hee hee hee—

 Florinda glares at her.

11

Hee hee—

She stops. Music continues under.

NARRATOR: Because the baker had lost his mother and father in a baking accident—well, at least that is what he believed—he was eager to have a family of his own, and concerned that all efforts until now had failed.

A knock on the Baker's door.

BAKER: Who might that be? (*He looks off to see*)
WIFE: We have sold our last loaf of bread . . .
BAKER: It's the witch from next door.

The Witch enters; music resumes.

WIFE, BAKER: We have no bread.
WITCH: Of course you have no bread!
BAKER: What do you wish?
WITCH: It's not what I wish. It's what *you* wish. (*Points to Wife's belly*) Nothing cooking in there now, is there?
NARRATOR: The old enchantress went on to tell the couple that she had placed a spell on their house.
BAKER: What spell?
WITCH: In the past, when you were no more than a babe, your father brought his young wife and you to this cottage. They were a handsome couple, but not handsome neighbors. You see, your mother was with child and she had developed an unusual appetite. She took one look at my beautiful garden and told your father that what she wanted more than anything in the world was

Greens, greens, and nothing but greens:
Parsley, peppers, cabbages and celery,
Asparagus and watercress and
Fiddleferns and lettuce—!
    (*Falling into "rap" style*)
He said, "All right,"
But it wasn't, quite,
'Cause I caught him in the autumn
In my garden one night!
He was robbing me,
Raping me,

Rooting through my rutabaga,
Raiding my arugula and
Ripping up the rampion
(My champion! My favorite!) —
I should have laid a spell on him
    (*"Spell" chord*)
Right there,
Could have turned him into stone
Or a dog or a chair
Or a sn—
    (*Drifts off into a momentary trance*)
But I let him have the rampion—
I'd lots to spare.
In return, however,
I said, "Fair is fair:
You can let me have the baby
That your wife will bear.

And we'll call it square."

Music stops.

BAKER: I had a brother?

WITCH: No. But you had a sister.

NARRATOR: But the witch refused to tell him any more of his
    sister. Not even that her name was Rapunzel. She
    went on:

Music resumes.

WITCH: I thought I had been more than reasonable, and that
    we all might live happily ever after. But how was I to
    know what your father had also hid in his pocket?!
    You see, when I had inherited that garden, my
    mother had warned me I would be punished if I ever
    were to lose any of the

    Beans.

BAKER, WIFE:
    Beans?

WITCH:
    The special beans.
        (*Getting worked up*)

13

INTO THE WOODS

I let him go,
I didn't know
He'd stolen my beans!
I was watching him crawl
Back over the wall—!
  ("*Rap*")
And then bang! Crash!
And the lightning flash!
And—well, that's another story,
Never mind—
Anyway, at last
The big day came
And I made my claim.
"Oh, don't take away the baby,"
They shrieked and screeched,
But I did,
And I hid her
Where she'll never be reached.

And your father cried,
And your mother died
When for extra measure—
I admit it was a pleasure—
I said, "Sorry,
I'm still not mollified."

And I laid a little spell on them—
  ("*Spell*" chord)
You too, son—
That your family tree
Would always be
A barren one . . .

Witch levitates in her chair, laughing as she goes;
Baker and Wife gasp in disbelief.

So there's no more fuss
And there's no more scenes
And my garden thrives—
You should see my nectarines!
But I'm telling you the same
I tell Kings and Queens:

14

Don't ever never ever
Mess around with my greens!
Especially the beans.

*Her chair returns to the ground; music continues
under; Jack has his cap and coat on.*

JACK'S MOTHER: Now listen to me, Jack. Lead Milky-White to
market and fetch the best price you can. Take no less
than five pounds. Are you listening to me?
JACK: Yes.
JACK'S MOTHER: Now how much are you to ask?
JACK: No more than five pounds.

She pinches his ear hard.

JACK'S MOTHER, JACK: Less! Than five.

She lets go.

JACK'S MOTHER:
Jack Jack Jack,
Head in a sack,
The house is getting colder,
This is not a time for dreaming.

Chimney-stack
Starting to crack,
The mice are getting bolder,
The floor's gone slack.
Your mother's getting older,
Your father's not back,
And you can't just sit here dreaming pretty dreams.

To wish and wait
From day to day
Will never keep
The wolves away.

So into the woods,
The time is now.
We have to live,
I don't care how.
Into the woods
To sell the cow,

15

You must begin the journey.
Straight through the woods
And don't delay—
We have to face
The marketplace.
Into the woods to journey's end—

JACK:

Into the woods to sell a friend—

Music continues under.

JACK'S MOTHER: Someday you'll have a real pet, Jack.
JACK: A piggy?

Mother shakes her head in disbelief.

NARRATOR: Meanwhile, the witch, for purposes of her own,
explained how the baker might lift the spell:

WITCH:

You wish to have
The curse reversed?
I'll need a certain
Potion first.

Go to the wood and bring me back
One: the cow as white as milk,
Two: the cape as red as blood,
Three: the hair as yellow as corn,
Four: the slipper as pure as gold.

Bring me these
Before the chime
Of midnight
In three days' time,
And you shall have,
I guarantee,
A child as perfect
As child can be.

Go to the wood!

She disappears. Fanfare.

16

STEPMOTHER: Ladies.

> *Fanfare.*

> Our carriage waits.

> *Cinderella shows her the plate of lentils.*

CINDERELLA:
> Now may I go to the Festival?

STEPMOTHER:
> The *Festival*—!
> Darling, those nails!
> Darling, those clothes!
> Lentils are one thing but
> Darling, with those,
> You'd make us the fools of the Festival
> And mortify the Prince!

> *Cinderella's Father enters.*

CINDERELLA'S FATHER:
> The carriage is waiting.

STEPMOTHER:
> We must be gone.

> *They exit with a flourish.*

CINDERELLA: Good night, Father.

> *He grunts and exits.*

> I wish . . .

> *Cinderella sits dejected, crying. Music continues under. The Baker, having gone off, returns in hunting gear.*

BAKER: Look what I found in Father's hunting jacket.
WIFE: Six beans.
BAKER: I wonder if they are the—
WIFE: Witch's beans? We'll take them with us.
BAKER: No! You are not coming.
WIFE: I know you are fearful of the woods at night.

BAKER:

> The spell is on *my* house.
> Only I can lift the spell,
> The spell is on *my* house.

WIFE (*Overlapping*):

> No, no, the spell is on *our* house.
> We must lift the spell together,
> The spell is on *our* house.

BAKER (*Overlapping*): No. You are not to come and that is final.
Now what am I to return with?
WIFE (*Annoyed*): You don't remember?

> The cow as white as milk,
> The cape as red as blood,
> The hair as yellow as corn,
> The slipper as pure as gold—

BAKER (*Memorizing*):

> The cow as white as milk,
> The cape as red as blood,
> The hair as yellow as corn,
> The slipper as pure as gold . . .

NARRATOR (*Overlapping*): And so the baker, reluctantly, set off
to meet the enchantress's demands. As for Cinderella:

CINDERELLA:

> I still wish to go to the Festival,
> But how am I ever to get to the Festival?

BAKER (*Simultaneously, muttering as he gets ready to leave*):

> The cow as white as milk,
> The cape as red as blood,
> The hair as yellow as corn—

WIFE (*Prompting*):

> The slipper—

BAKER:

> The slipper as pure as gold . . .

CINDERELLA (*Overlapping*):
>I know!
>I'll visit Mother's grave,
>The grave at the hazel tree,
>And tell her I just want to
>Go to the King's Festival . . .

BAKER:
>The cow, the cape,
>The slipper as pure as gold—

WIFE:
>The hair—!

BAKER, CINDERELLA:
>Into the woods,
>It's time to go,
>It may be all
>In vain, you (I) know.
>Into the woods—
>But even so,
>I have to take the journey.

BAKER, CINDERELLA, WIFE:
>Into the woods,
>The path is straight,
>You (I) know it well,
>But who can tell—?

BAKER, WIFE:
>Into the woods to lift the spell—

CINDERELLA:
>Into the woods to visit Mother—

WIFE:
>Into the woods to fetch the things—

BAKER:
>To make the potion—

CINDERELLA:
>To go to the Festival—

BAKER, WIFE, CINDERELLA, JACK, JACK'S MOTHER:
> Into the woods
> Without regret,
> The choice is made,
> The task is set.
> Into the woods,
> But not forget-
> Ting why I'm (you're) on the journey.
>
> Into the woods
> To get my (our) wish,
> I don't care how,
> The time is now.

JACK'S MOTHER:
> Into the woods to sell the cow—

JACK:
> Into the woods to get the money—
>> (*Leads Milky-White into the woods*)

WIFE:
> Into the woods to lift the spell—

BAKER:
> To make the potion—
>> (*He sets off for the woods*)

CINDERELLA:
> To go to the Festival—
>> (*She sets off for the woods*)

LITTLE RED RIDINGHOOD (*Skipping by*):
> Into the woods to Grandmother's house . . .
> Into the woods to Grandmother's house . . .

ALL:
> The way is clear,
> The light is good,
> I have no fear,
> Nor no one should.
> The woods are just trees,
> The trees are just wood.
> No need to be afraid there—

BAKER, CINDERELLA (*Apprehensive*):
>There's something in the glade there . . .

*Cinderella's Father, Stepmother and stepsisters are
seen riding in their carriage.*

ALL:
>Into the woods
>Without delay,
>But careful not
>To lose the way.
>Into the woods,
>Who knows what may
>Be lurking on the journey?
>
>Into the woods
>To get the thing
>That makes it worth
>The journeying.
>Into the woods—

STEPMOTHER, STEPSISTERS:
>To see the King—

JACK, JACK'S MOTHER:
>To sell the cow—

BAKER, WIFE:
>To make the potion—

ALL:
>To see—
>To sell—
>To get—
>To bring—
>To make—
>To lift—
>To go to the Festival—!
>
>Into the woods!
>Into the woods!
>Into the woods,
>Then out of the woods,
>And home before dark!

Scene 2

The woods. Late afternoon.
The stage is filled by trees of all varieties, many twisted and gnarled, others going straight forward to the sky without a branch. Bright sunlight streams through, creating a wonderful light-maze. As the scene progresses, the sunlight is gradually replaced by moonlight. The foliage rustles in the breeze, with an occasional gust blowing about low-lying fog.
Cinderella enters and kneels before a tree filled with birds.

NARRATOR: Cinderella had planted a branch at the grave of her mother and she visited there so often, and wept so much, that her tears watered it until it had become a handsome tree.

CINDERELLA:
I've been good and I've been kind, Mother,
Doing only what I learned from you.
Why then am I left behind, Mother,
Is there something more that I should do?
What is wrong with me, Mother?
Something must be wrong.
I wish—

Suddenly, the ghost of Cinderella's Mother appears within the tree.

CINDERELLA'S MOTHER: What, child? Specify. Opportunity is not a lengthy visitor and good fortune, like bad, can befall when least expected.

CINDERELLA:
I wish . . .

CINDERELLA'S MOTHER:
Do you know what you wish?
Are you certain what you wish
Is what you want?
If you know what you want,
Then make a wish.

Ask the tree,
And you shall have your wish.

CINDERELLA:

Shiver and quiver, little tree.
Silver and gold throw down on me.

*A gold-and-silver dress and fancy slippers drop
from the tree.*

I'm off to get my wish.

*Cinderella picks up the clothes and dashes off. Jack
is walking through the woods. He leads Milky-
White. He stops.*

JACK: Quiet. Silence everywhere, Milky-White. Not to my
liking . . .

Pause. Music fades out.

MYSTERIOUS MAN (*Steps from behind a tree*): Hello, Jack.
JACK: How did you know my name?!
MYSTERIOUS MAN: When first I appear I seem mysterious. But
when explained, I am nothing serious.
JACK: Say that again.
MYSTERIOUS MAN: On your way to market? You might have
been there long ago. Taking your time, Jack?
JACK: No, sir.
MYSTERIOUS MAN: Is that the truth?
JACK: Well, you see, now I'm *resting*—
MYSTERIOUS MAN: How much are you asking for the animal?
JACK: No less than five pounds, sir.
MYSTERIOUS MAN: Oh now, Jack. Why such a sum?
JACK: My mother told me—
MYSTERIOUS MAN: Your mother? A boy your age? Why you'd be
lucky to exchange her for a sack of beans.
JACK: Well, I—

*Before Jack can respond, the Mysterious Man has
disappeared.*

Come along, Milky-White. There are spirits here . . .
(*He exits*)

*Another part of the woods. Little Red Ridinghood,
skipping to the accompaniment of ''Into the
Woods,'' is surprised by the Wolf. Music stops.*

WOLF: Good day, young lady.
LITTLE RED RIDINGHOOD: Good day, Mr. Wolf.

*Music resumes, Little Red Ridinghood continues.
Wolf stops her again. Music stops.*

WOLF: Whither away so hurriedly?
LITTLE RED RIDINGHOOD: To my grandmother's.

*Music resumes; Little Red Ridinghood continues
briefly. Wolf stops her once more.*

WOLF: And what might be in your basket?
LITTLE RED RIDINGHOOD: Bread and wine, so Grandmother will
    have something good to make her strong.
WOLF: And where might your grandmother live?

Baker appears behind a tree and eavesdrops.

LITTLE RED RIDINGHOOD: A good quarter of a league further in
    the woods; her house stands under three large oak
    trees.

*Wolf grunts lasciviously, sings to himself as he
watches her skip off.*

WOLF:

Mmmh . . .
    (*Rubbing his thighs*)
Unhh . . .

Look at that flesh,
Pink and plump.
    (*To himself*)
Hello, little girl . . .

Tender and fresh,
Not one lump.
Hello, little girl . . .

This one's especially lush,
Delicious . . .
Mmmh . . .

(*Smacks his lips, then runs over and pops up in front of
Little Red Ridinghood*)
Hello, little girl,
What's your rush?
You're missing all the flowers.
The sun won't set for hours,
Take your time.

LITTLE RED RIDINGHOOD:
Mother said,
"Straight ahead,"
Not to delay
Or be misled.

WOLF:
But slow, little girl,
Hark! And hush—
The birds are singing sweetly.
You'll miss the birds completely,
You're traveling so fleetly.

*Little Red Ridinghood stops to listen; the Wolf
devours her with his eyes, mutters to himself.*

Grandmother first,
Then Miss Plump . . .
What a delectable couple:
Utter perfection
One brittle, one supple—
(*Seeing Little Red Ridinghood start to move off again*)
One moment, my dear—!

Little Red Ridinghood stops again.

LITTLE RED RIDINGHOOD:
Mother said,
"Come what may,
Follow the path
And never stray."

WOLF:
Just so, little girl—
Any path.
So many worth exploring.

25

Just one would be so boring.
And look what you're ignoring . . .

*He gestures to the trees and flowers; Little Red
Ridinghood looks around.*

   (*To himself*)
Think of those crisp,
Aging bones,
Then something fresh on the palate.
Think of that scrumptious carnality
Twice in one day—!
There's no possible way
To describe what you feel
When you're talking to your meal!

*The Baker enters, but hides behind a tree at the
sight of the Wolf.*

LITTLE RED RIDINGHOOD:
     Mother said
     Not to stray.
     Still, I suppose,
     A small delay . . .
     Granny might like
     A fresh bouquet . . .

     Goodbye, Mr. Wolf.

WOLF:
     Goodbye, little girl.
     And hello . . .

He howls and exits in the direction of the cottage.

BAKER (*Horrified*): Is harm to come to that little girl . . . in the
red cape!

*Witch surprises him as she hangs from a tree;
music under.*

WITCH: Forget the little girl and get the cape!
BAKER (*Clutching his chest*): You frightened me.
WITCH (*Nasty*): That's the cape. Get it. Get it. Get it!
BAKER: How am I supposed to get it?

WITCH: You go up to the little thing, and you take it.

BAKER: I can't just take a cloak from a little girl. Why don't you take it!

WITCH: If I could, I would! But I—

We suddenly hear Rapunzel singing in the distance.

(*Sweetly*) Ahh, my Rapunzel . . . listen to her beautiful music . . . (*Yelling*) Get me what I need. Get me what I need! (*She disappears back up into the tree*)

BAKER (*Distraught*): This is ridiculous. I'll never get that red cape, nor find a golden cow, or a yellow slipper—or was it a golden slipper and a yellow cow? Oh, no . . .

Wife appears.

WIFE:

> The cow as white as milk,
> The cape as red as blood,
> The hair as yellow as corn,
> The slipper as pure as—

BAKER (*Overlapping*): What are you doing here?

WIFE (*Takes a scarf and tries to put it around his neck*): You forgot your scarf—

BAKER (*Taking scarf off*): You have no business being alone in the woods. And you have no idea what I've come upon here. You would be frightened for your life. Now go home immediately!

WIFE: I wish to help.

BAKER: No!

> The spell is on *my* house—

WIFE:

> *Our* house.

BAKER:

> Only I can lift the spell,
> The spell is on *my* house—!

WIFE (*Overlapping*):

> We must lift the spell together,
> The spell is on—

27

She puts her hand across his mouth; we see Jack at the other side of the stage.

A cow as white as—

She takes her hand away; music stops.

BAKER, WIFE: —milk.

Wife pushes Baker in Jack's direction; she follows.

BAKER: Hello there, young man.

JACK: Hello, sir.

BAKER: What might you be doing with a cow in the middle of the forest?

JACK (*Nervous*): I was heading toward market—but I seem to have lost my way.

WIFE (*Coaching Baker*): What are you planning to do there—?

BAKER: And what are you planning to do there?

JACK: Sell my cow, sir. No less than five pounds.

BAKER: Five pounds! (*To Wife*) Where am I to get five pounds!

WIFE (*Taking over*): She must be generous of milk to fetch five pounds?

JACK (*Hesitant*): Yes, ma'am.

WIFE: And if you can't fetch that sum? Then what are you to do?

JACK: I hadn't thought of that . . . . I suppose my mother and I will have no food to eat.

Baker has emptied his pocket; he has a few coins and the beans in hand.

BAKER (*To Wife*): This is the sum total . . .

WIFE (*Loudly*): Beans—we mustn't give up our beans! Well . . . if you feel we must.

BAKER: Huh?

WIFE (*To Jack*): Beans *will* bring you food, son.

JACK: Beans in exchange for my cow?

WIFE: Oh, these are no ordinary beans, son. These beans carry magic.

JACK: Magic? What kind of magic?

WIFE (*To Baker*): Tell him.

Mysterious Man enters behind a tree.

28

BAKER (*Nervous*): Magic that defies description.

JACK: My mother would—

MYSTERIOUS MAN: You'd be lucky to exchange her for a sack of beans. (*He exits before anyone sees him*)

JACK: How many beans?

BAKER: Six.

WIFE: Five! We can't part with all of them. We must leave one for ourselves. Besides, I'd say they're worth a pound each, at the very least.

JACK: Could I buy my cow back someday?

BAKER (*Uneasy*): Well . . . possibly.

> *He hands Jack the beans, counting out five and keeping one for his pocket; Wife then takes the cow; music.*

Good luck there, young lad.

JACK (*Tearful; to the cow*):
> I guess this is goodbye, old pal.
> You've been a perfect friend.
> I hate to see us part, old pal,
> Someday I'll buy you back.
> I'll see you soon again.
> I hope that when I do,
> It won't be on a plate.

> *Overcome with emotion, Jack leaves; music continues under.*

BAKER (*Angry*): Take the cow and go home!

WIFE: I was trying to be helpful.

BAKER: Magic beans! We've no reason to believe they're magic! Are we to dispel this curse through deceit?

WIFE: No one would have given him more for that creature. We did him a favor. At least they'll have some food.

BAKER: Five beans!

WIFE:
> If you know
> What you want,
> Then you go
> And you find it
> And you get it—

BAKER (*Pointing off*): Home.
WIFE: Do we want a child or not?

> —and you give
> And you take
> And you bid
> And you bargain,
> Or you live
> To regret it.

BAKER: Will you please go home.
WIFE:

> There are rights and wrongs
> And in-betweens—
> No one waits
> When fortune intervenes.
> And maybe they're really magic.
> Who knows?
>
> Why you do
> What you do,
> That's the point,
> All the rest of it
> Is chatter.

BAKER (*Gesturing toward Milky-White*): Look at her, she's crying.
WIFE:

> If the thing you do
> Is pure in intent,
> If it's meant,
> And it's just a little bent,
> Does it matter?

BAKER: Yes.
WIFE:

> No, what matters is that
> Everyone tells tiny lies—
> What's important, really, is the size.
>   (*Pause; no response*)
> Only three more tries
> And we'll have our prize.
> When the end's in sight,

30

You'll realize:
If the end is right,
It justifies
The beans!

BAKER: Take the cow and go home. I will carry this out in my own fashion!

Wife and Baker exit in different directions. Rapunzel is heard singing off in the distance. Her tower appears; music continues.

NARRATOR: And so the baker continued his search for the cape as red as blood. As for Rapunzel, the witch was careful not to lose this beauty to the outside world, and so shut her within a doorless tower. And when the old enchantress paid a visit, she called forth:

WITCH: Rapunzel. Rapunzel. Let down your hair to me.

Rapunzel stops singing and her hair descends. The Witch, with great difficulty, and with great pain to Rapunzel, climbs up her hair; Rapunzel's Prince comes from around a tree.

RAPUNZEL'S PRINCE (*To himself*): Rapunzel, Rapunzel. What a strange name. Strange but beautiful . . . and fit for a Prince. Tomorrow, before that horrible witch arrives, I will stand before her window and ask her to let down her hair to *me*.

Another part of the woods. The Baker steps into Little Red Ridinghood's path; the girl is eating a sweet.

BAKER: Hello there, little one.
LITTLE RED RIDINGHOOD: Hello.
BAKER: Have you saved some of those sweets for Granny?
LITTLE RED RIDINGHOOD (*Embarrassed*): I ate all the sweets, *and* half the loaf of bread.
BAKER: Where did you get that beautiful cape? I so admire it.
LITTLE RED RIDINGHOOD: My granny made it for me.
BAKER: Is that right? I would love a red cloak like that.
LITTLE RED RIDINGHOOD (*Giggling*): You'd look pretty foolish.

31

Baker goes to her and grabs her cape.

BAKER: May I take a look at it?

LITTLE RED RIDINGHOOD (*In panic*): I don't like to be without my cape. Please, give it back!

BAKER (*Frustrated*): I want it badly.

LITTLE RED RIDINGHOOD: Give it back, please!

WITCH'S VOICE: Forget the little girl and get the cape!

Baker suddenly dashes away with the cape under his arm. Little Red Ridinghood stands numb for a moment, then lets out a bloodcurdling scream, followed by hysterical weeping.

BAKER (*Sheepishly returning with cape, placing it on Little Red Ridinghood's shoulders*): I just wanted to make certain that you *really* loved this cape. Now you go to your granny's—and you be careful that no wolf comes your way.

LITTLE RED RIDINGHOOD: I'd rather a wolf than you, any day.

She stomps hard on the Baker's toe and exits.

BAKER (*In pain*):
> If you know
> What you need,
> Then you go
> And you find it
> And you take it—
> Do I want a child or not?
>
> (*Feeling stronger*)
> It's a cloak,
> What's a cloak?
> It's a joke,
> It's a stupid little cloak.
> And a cloak is what you make it.
> (*Nods, convincing himself*)
> So you take it.
>
> (*With resolve*)
> Things are only what you need them for,
> What's important is who needs them more—

Sondheim & Lapine

Music continues under as he exits.

NARRATOR: And so the baker, with newfound determination, went after the red cape. As for the little girl, she was surprised to find her grandmother's cottage door standing open.

We see Granny's cottage. The walls are made of scrim. Little Red Ridinghood enters. The Wolf, dressed as Granny, is in the bed.

LITTLE RED RIDINGHOOD (*To herself*): Oh, dear. How uneasy I feel. Perhaps it's all the sweets. (*Towards the bed*) Good day, Grandmother. (*Moves to the bed*) My, Grandmother, you're looking *very* strange. What big ears you have!

WOLF (*In a Granny voice*): The better to hear you with, my dear.

LITTLE RED RIDINGHOOD: But Grandmother, what big eyes you have!

WOLF: The better to see you with, my dear.

LITTLE RED RIDINGHOOD: But Grandmother, what large hands you have!

WOLF: The better to hug you with, my dear.

LITTLE RED RIDINGHOOD: Oh, Grandmother. What a terrible, big, wet mouth you have!

WOLF: The better to eat you with!

Bloodcurdling scream from Little Red Ridinghood as lights fade to black.

NARRATOR: And scarcely had the wolf said this, than with a single bound he was devouring the little girl. Well, it was a full day of eating for both. And with his appetite appeased, the wolf took to bed for a nice long nap.

Wolf snores; Baker is outside cottage.

BAKER: That grandmother has a mighty snore. (*He goes up to the window and looks in*) Odd. Where is the little one? Eating, no doubt.

Baker turns to walk away; Wolf belches; Baker suddenly stops.

Or eaten!

33

Baker enters the house and timidly goes over to the bed, his knife stretched before him. He lets out a yelp when he sees the Wolf with his swollen belly.

Grandmother, hah! (*He draws the knife back, then stops*) What is this red cloth in the corner of your mouth? Looks to me to be a piece of—ah-hah! I'll get the cape from within your stomach.

He slits the Wolf's stomach, then recoils in disgust.

LITTLE RED RIDINGHOOD (*Stepping out of the Wolf, bloodied*): What a fright! How dark and dank it was inside that wolf.

Granny emerges from Wolf.

GRANNY (*Wheezing*): Kill the devil! Take that knife and cut his evil head off! Let's see the demon sliced into a thousand bits. Better yet, let the animal die a painful, agonizing, hideous death.

LITTLE RED RIDINGHOOD (*Shocked*): Granny!

GRANNY: Quiet, child. This evil needs to be destroyed. Fetch me some great stones! We'll fill his belly with them, then we'll watch him try to run away!

BAKER (*Faint*): Well, I will leave you to your task.

GRANNY: Don't you want the skins?

BAKER: No. No! You keep them.

GRANNY (*With disdain*): What kind of a hunter are you?

BAKER: I'm a baker!

Granny pulls him into the house as Little Red Ridinghood walks downstage, as if to gather stones. Lights change; music.

LITTLE RED RIDINGHOOD:
> Mother said,
> "Straight ahead,"
> Not to delay
> Or be misled.
> I should have heeded
> Her advice . . .

> But he seemed so nice.

And he showed me things,
Many beautiful things,
That I hadn't thought to explore.
They were off my path,
So I never had dared.
I had been so careful
I never had cared.
And he made me feel excited—
Well, excited and scared.

When he said, "Come in!"
With that sickening grin,
How could I know what was in store?
Once his teeth were bared,
Though, I really got scared—
Well, excited and scared—

But he drew me close
And he swallowed me down,
Down a dark slimy path
Where lie secrets that I never want to know,
And when everything familiar
Seemed to disappear forever,
At the end of the path
Was Granny once again.

So we wait in the dark
Until someone sets us free,
And we're brought into the light,
And we're back at the start.

And I know things now,
Many valuable things,
That I hadn't known before:
Do not put your faith
In a cape and a hood—
They will not protect you
The way that they should—
And take extra care with strangers,
Even flowers have their dangers.
And though scary is exciting,
Nice is different than good.

Now I know:
Don't be scared.
Granny is right,
Just be prepared.

Isn't it nice to know a lot!

. . . and a little bit not . . .

*Baker crosses stage. Little Red Ridinghood crosses
to him.*

Mr. Baker, you saved our lives. Here. (*She hands him
her cape*)

BAKER: Are you certain?

LITTLE RED RIDINGHOOD: Yes. Maybe Granny will make me another with the skins of that wolf.

BAKER: Thank you.

They exit in different directions.

NARRATOR: And so the baker, with the second article in hand,
feeling braver and more satisfied than he had ever
felt, ran back through the woods.

A cutout of Jack's house appears.

As for the lad Jack:

*Jack's mother and Jack come from behind the cut-
out.*

JACK'S MOTHER (*Livid*): Only a dolt would exchange a cow for
beans! (*She throws the beans to the ground*)

JACK: Mother, no— (*He goes to pick them up*)

JACK'S MOTHER: To bed without supper for you!

*She grabs the boy and marches him into the house
as it goes offstage.*

NARRATOR: Little did they know those beans would grow into
an enormous stalk that would stretch into the
heavens.

*Music; Wife enters upstage tugging at Milky-
White. Ball music in the distance, growing louder.*

Cinderella dashes onstage, looking over her shoulder. She falls; music stops.

WIFE: Are you all right, miss?

CINDERELLA (*Breathless*): Yes. I just need to catch my breath.

WIFE: What a beautiful gown you're wearing. Were you at the King's Festival?

CINDERELLA (*Preoccupied*): Yes.

WIFE: Aren't you the lucky one. Why ever are you in the woods at this hour?

Fanfares in the distance, growing louder. We hear men's voices offstage. Cinderella signals to Wife to keep quiet, then ducks behind a tree. Cinderella's Prince runs onstage, followed by his Steward. They look about for a moment, then notice Wife.

CINDERELLA'S PRINCE: Have you seen a beautiful young woman in a ball gown pass through?

Wife bows.

WIFE (*Breathless*): I don't think so, sir.

STEWARD: I think I see her over there.

Cinderella's Prince signals him off in that direction, then takes another look at Wife before following. Music continues under.

WIFE: I've never lied to royalty before. I've never *anything* to royalty before!

CINDERELLA: Thank you.

WIFE: If a Prince were looking for me, I certainly wouldn't hide.

CINDERELLA (*Defensive*): Well, what brings *you* here—and with a cow?

WIFE: Oh, my husband's somewhere in the woods. (*Proud*) He's undoing a spell.

CINDERELLA (*Impressed*): Oh?

WIFE: Oh, yes. Now, the Prince, what was he like?

CINDERELLA:
He's a very nice Prince.

WIFE:

    And—?

CINDERELLA:

    And—
    It's a very nice Ball.

WIFE:

    And—?

CINDERELLA:

    And—
    When I entered, they trumpeted.

WIFE:

    And—?
    The Prince—?

CINDERELLA:

    Oh, the Prince . . .

WIFE:

    Yes, the Prince!

CINDERELLA:

    Well, he's tall.

WIFE:

    Is that all?
    Did you dance?
    Is he charming? They say that he's charming.

CINDERELLA:

    We did nothing *but* dance.

WIFE:

    Yes—? And—?

CINDERELLA:

    And it made a nice change.

WIFE:

    No, the Prince!

CINDERELLA

    Oh, the Prince . . .

WIFE:
> Yes, the Prince.

CINDERELLA:
> He has charm for a Prince, I guess . . .

WIFE:
> Guess?

CINDERELLA:
> I don't meet a wide range.
> And it's all very strange.

WIFE: Are you to return to the Festival tomorrow eve?
CINDERELLA: Perhaps.
WIFE: Perhaps? Oh, to be pursued by a Prince. All that pursues me is tomorrow's bread.

We hear the first chime of midnight.

What I wouldn't give to be in your shoes.

Second chime; chimes continue under.

CINDERELLA: Will you look over there.

Milky-White stands and looks.

An enormous vine growing next to that little cottage.
WIFE (*Looking down at Cinderella's feet*): . . . I mean slippers.
CINDERELLA: It looks like a giant beanstalk rising into the sky.
WIFE (*Excited*): As pure as gold?
CINDERELLA: I must get home. (*Begins to leave*)
WIFE: Wait!

Cinderella exits.

I need your shoes!

Wife starts off after Cinderella; Milky-White lets out a "Moo!" and takes off in the other direction; Wife stops, torn between Milky-White and Cinderella.

WIFE (*To Cinderella*): Hey! (*To Milky-White*) Come back here!

Wife takes off after Milky-White; final chime of midnight; music continues under; one by one,

each of the characters appears moving through the woods, darting in and out of the trees and paths, pursuing their errands, mostly oblivious to one another.
The night turns gradually into dawn.
The following lines are spoken rhythmically as each character appears and disappears.

BAKER:
One midnight gone . . .

MYSTERIOUS MAN:
No knot unties itself . . .

WITCH:
Sometimes the things you most wish for
Are not to be touched . . .

PRINCES:
The harder to get, the better to have . . .

CINDERELLA'S PRINCE:
Agreed?

RAPUNZEL'S PRINCE:
Agreed.

FLORINDA:
Never wear mauve at a ball . . .

LUCINDA:
Or pink . . .

STEPMOTHER (*To stepdaughters*):
Or open your mouth . . .

JACK (*Looking up and off at the beanstalk*):
The difference between a cow and a bean
Is a bean can begin an adventure . . .

JACK'S MOTHER (*Looking off in Jack's direction*):
Slotted spoons don't hold much soup . . .

LITTLE RED RIDINGHOOD:
The prettier the flower, the farther from the path . . .

CINDERELLA'S FATHER:
> The closer to the family, the closer to the wine . . .

RAPUNZEL (*Offstage*):
> Ah-ah-ah-ah-ah . . .

WITCH (*Reappearing suddenly*):
> One midnight gone! . . .

GRANNY:
> The mouth of a wolf's not the end of the world . . .

STEWARD:
> A servant is not just a dog, to a Prince . . .

CINDERELLA:
> Opportunity is not a lengthy visitor . . .

WIFE:
> You may know what you need,
> But to get what you want,
> Better see that you keep what you have.

All sing, overlapping.

BAKER:
> One midnight gone . . .

WITCH:
> Sometimes the things you most wish for
> Are not to be touched . . .

PRINCES:
> The harder to get the better to have . . .

CINDERELLA'S PRINCE:
> Agreed?

RAPUNZEL'S PRINCE:
> Agreed.

BAKER:
> One midnight gone . . . one midnight gone . . .

FLORINDA:
> Never wear mauve at a ball . . .

LUCINDA:

> Or pink . . .

JACK'S MOTHER:

> Slotted spoons don't hold much soup . . .

BAKER'S WIFE:

> To get what you want better keep what you . . .

LITTLE RED RIDINGHOOD:

> The prettier the flower . . .

ALL:

> One midnight one midnight one midnight gone . . .
>
> Into the woods,
> Into the woods,
> Into the woods, then out of the woods
> And home before—

Scene 3

Baker sleeps beneath a tree.
Music; Jack appears suddenly from the trees, car-
rying an oversized money sack.

JACK:

> There are giants in the sky!
> There are big tall terrible giants in the sky!
>
> When you're way up high
> And you look below
> At the world you've left
> And the things you know,
> Little more than a glance
> Is enough to show
> You just how small you are.
>
> When you're way up high
> And you're on your own
> In a world like none
> That you've ever known,

Where the sky is lead
And the earth is stone,

You're free to do
Whatever pleases you,
Exploring things you'd never dare
'Cause you don't care,
When suddenly there's
A big tall terrible giant at the door,
A big tall terrible lady giant sweeping the floor.

And she gives you food
And she gives you rest
And she draws you close
To her giant breast,
And you know things now that you never knew be-
    fore,
Not till the sky.

Only just when you've made
A friend and all,
And you know she's big
But you don't feel small,
Someone bigger than her
Comes along the hall
To swallow you for lunch.

And your heart is lead
And your stomach stone
And you're really scared
Being all alone . . .

And it's then that you miss
All the things you've known
And the world you've left
And the little you own—

The fun is done.
You steal what you can and run!
And you scramble down
And you look below,
And the world you know
Begins to grow:

43

The roof, the house, and your mother at the door.
The roof, the house, and the world you never thought
　　to explore.
And you think of all of the things you've seen,
And you wish that you could live in between,
And you're back again,
Only different than before,
After the sky.

There are giants in the sky!
There are big tall terrible awesome scary wonderful
Giants in the sky!

Baker stirs; Jack bounds over to him.

JACK: Good fortune! Good fortune, sir! Look what I have!
　　Here's five gold pieces.
BAKER (*Astounded*): Five gold pieces! (*He examines the gold*)
JACK: I had more, but my mother made me surrender them.
　　She allowed me these five to do with as I pleased.
BAKER: Oh, my . . .
JACK: Where is Milky-White?
BAKER: Milky-White is back home with my wife.
JACK: Let's go find them! (*He grabs Baker and starts to pull him
　　away*)
BAKER: Wait! I don't know that I wish to sell.
JACK: But you said I might buy her back.
BAKER: I know, but I'm not certain that five gold pieces
　　would—
JACK: Are you saying that you wish more money?
BAKER: More money is always—
JACK (*Hands him gold*): Keep this. I will go fetch more.
BAKER: Wait. I didn't say—

Jack exits; Baker looks at money.

Five gold pieces! With this money I could buy baking
supplies for a year. I could buy a new thatched roof
and a new chimney.

Mysterious Man appears from nowhere.

MYSTERIOUS MAN: But could you buy yourself a child?
BAKER (*Startled*): Who are you?

44

MYSTERIOUS MAN: When first I appear I seem delirious. But when explained, I am nothing serious. Could you buy yourself a child?

BAKER: I don't understand.

MYSTERIOUS MAN: How badly do you wish a child? Five gold pieces? Ten? Twenty?

BAKER: I've not thought to put a price on it.

MYSTERIOUS MAN: Exactly. (*He walks over and distracts the Baker and takes the gold*) You've not thought about many things, have you son?

BAKER: Give me back the money! It is not yours—

MYSTERIOUS MAN: Nor is it Jack's. The money is not what's important. What's important is that your wish be honored.

Mysterious Man goes around a tree and disappears; Baker begins darting around trees looking for him.

BAKER: Come back here! Damn! Give me back—

He sees Wife, who comes from around another tree.

What are you doing here now?

WIFE (*Quickly switching gears*): I see you've the red cape.

BAKER: Yes. I've the cape. Only two items left to locate.

WIFE: Three.

BAKER: Two. I've the cape and the cow.

WIFE (*Faking enthusiasm*): You've the cape!

BAKER: WHAT HAVE YOU DONE WITH THE COW?!

WIFE: She ran away. I never reached home. I've been looking for her all night.

BAKER: I should have known better than to have entrusted her to you.

WIFE: She might just as easily have run from you!

BAKER: But she didn't!

WIFE: BUT SHE MIGHT HAVE!

BAKER: BUT SHE DIDN'T!!!

Witch appears from nowhere.

WITCH: WHO CARES! THE COW IS GONE! GET IT BACK! *GET IT BACK!!!*

All three settle down.

BAKER (*Walks over to Witch*): We were just going to do that. (*Offers cape*) Here. I can give you this—
WITCH: DON'T GIVE ME THAT, FOOL!! I don't want to touch that! Have you no sense?

Rapunzel is heard suddenly, singing in the background.

My sweetness calls. (*Tough*) By tomorrow's midnight—deliver the items or you'll wish you never thought to have a child!

Witch zaps them with lightning and leaves.

BAKER: I don't like that woman.
WIFE (*Contrite*): I'm sorry I lost the cow.
BAKER: I shouldn't have yelled. (*Beat*) Now, please, go back to the village.

Wife, annoyed, turns her back and begins to walk away.

I *will* make things right. And then we can just go about our life. No more hunting about in the woods for strange objects. No more witches and dimwitted boys and hungry little girls.

Wife begins to move back towards him.

Go!

They exit in opposite directions.
Two fanfares. Another part of the forest. Cinderella's Prince, somewhat bedraggled, crosses the stage. He is met by Rapunzel's Prince.

RAPUNZEL'S PRINCE: Ah, there you are, good brother. Father and I had wondered where you had gone.
CINDERELLA'S PRINCE: I have been looking all night . . . for her.
RAPUNZEL'S PRINCE: Her?
CINDERELLA'S PRINCE: The beautiful one I danced the evening with.
RAPUNZEL'S PRINCE: Where did she go?

*Wife begins walking by; noticing the Princes, she
hides behind a tree and eavesdrops.*

CINDERELLA'S PRINCE: Disappeared, like the fine morning mist.

RAPUNZEL'S PRINCE: She was lovely.

CINDERELLA'S PRINCE: The loveliest.

RAPUNZEL'S PRINCE: I am not certain of that! I must confess, I too have found a lovely maiden. She lives here in the woods.

CINDERELLA'S PRINCE (*Incredulous*): The woods?

RAPUNZEL'S PRINCE: Yes! In the top of a tall tower that has no door or stairs.

CINDERELLA'S PRINCE: Where?

RAPUNZEL'S PRINCE: Two leagues from here, due east, just beyond the mossy knoll.

CINDERELLA'S PRINCE: And how do you manage a visit?

RAPUNZEL'S PRINCE: I stand beneath her tower and say, "Rapunzel, Rapunzel, let down your hair to me." And then she lowers the longest, most beautiful head of hair—yellow as corn—which I climb to her.

Wife reacts.

CINDERELLA'S PRINCE (*Starts laughing hysterically*): Rapunzel, Rapunzel! What kind of name is that? You jest! I have never heard of such a thing.

RAPUNZEL'S PRINCE (*Defensive*): I speak the truth! She is as true as your maiden. A maiden running from a Prince? None would run from us.

CINDERELLA'S PRINCE (*Sober*): Yet one has.

Music.

Did I abuse her
Or show her disdain?
Why does she run from me?
If I should lose her,
How shall I regain
The heart she has won from me?

Agony!
Beyond power of speech,
When the one thing you want
Is the only thing out of your reach.

47

RAPUNZEL'S PRINCE:
> High in her tower,
> She sits by the hour,
> Maintaining her hair.
> Blithe and becoming,
> And frequently humming
> A lighthearted air:
> > (*Hums Rapunzel's theme*)
> Ah-ah-ah-ah-ah-ah-ah—
> Agony!
> Far more painful than yours,
> When you know she would go with you,
> If there only were doors.

BOTH:
> Agony!
> Oh the torture they teach!

RAPUNZEL'S PRINCE:
> What's as intriguing—

CINDERELLA'S PRINCE:
> Or half so fatiguing—

BOTH:
> As what's out of reach?

CINDERELLA'S PRINCE:
> Am I not sensitive, clever,
> Well-mannered, considerate,
> Passionate, charming,
> As kind as I'm handsome,
> And heir to a throne?

RAPUNZEL'S PRINCE:
> You are everything maidens could wish for!

CINDERELLA'S PRINCE:
> Then why no—?

RAPUNZEL'S PRINCE:
> Do I know?

CINDERELLA'S PRINCE:
> The girl must be mad!

RAPUNZEL'S PRINCE:
> You know nothing of madness
> Till you're climbing her hair
> And you see her up there
> As you're nearing her,
> All the while hearing her
> "Ah-ah-ah-ah-ah-ah-ah-ah-ah-ah-ah-ah—"

BOTH:
> Agony!

CINDERELLA'S PRINCE:
> Misery!

RAPUNZEL'S PRINCE:
> Woe!

BOTH:
> Though it's different for each.

CINDERELLA'S PRINCE:
> Always ten steps behind—

RAPUNZEL'S PRINCE:
> Always ten feet below—

BOTH:
> And she's just out of reach.
> Agony
> That can cut like a knife!
>
> I must have her to wife.
>
> *They exit.*

WIFE: *Two* Princes, each more handsome than the other. (*She begins to follow the Princes; she stops*) No! Get the hair! (*She heads in the other direction*)

Jack's Mother enters frantically; music fades.

JACK'S MOTHER: Excuse me, young woman. Have you encountered a boy with carrot-top hair and a sunny, though occasionally vague, disposition, answering to the name of Jack?
WIFE: Not the one partial to a white cow?
JACK'S MOTHER: He's the one.

WIFE: Have you seen the cow?

JACK'S MOTHER: No, and I don't care to ever again. (*Confidential*) Children can be very queer about their animals. You be careful with your children . . .

WIFE: I have no children.

> *Beat.*

JACK'S MOTHER: That's okay, too.

WIFE: Yes . . . well, I've not seen your son today.

JACK'S MOTHER (*Annoyed*): I hope he didn't go up that beanstalk again. Quit while you're ahead, *I* say. (*She begins to exit*) Jack . . . ! Jack . . . !

> *Wife, after a moment's pause, exits in the other direction; Baker enters looking for the cow.*

BAKER (*Forlorn*): Moo . . . . Moo . . .

> *Mysterious Man appears from nowhere.*

MYSTERIOUS MAN: Moo! Looking for your cow?

> *Mysterious Man signals offstage and Milky-White enters.*

BAKER: Where did you find her?

> *Mysterious Man ducks back behind a tree as Baker goes to cow. He turns, and sees the old man is gone.*

Hello?

> *Baker takes cow and exits. Mysterious Man reappears and watches after Baker. Witch surprises him.*

WITCH: What are you doing?

MYSTERIOUS MAN: I am here to make amends.

WITCH: I want you to stay out of this, old man!

MYSTERIOUS MAN: I am here to see your wish is granted.

WITCH: You've caused enough trouble! Keep out of my path!

> *Witch zaps Mysterious Man; he runs off; she follows him; Wife approaches Rapunzel's tower.*

WIFE (*To herself*): I hope there are no witches to encounter. (*Calling up*) Rapunzel, Rapunzel? Let your hair down to me.

RAPUNZEL (*Dubious*): Is that you, my Prince?

WIFE (*In a deep voice*): Yes.

> *Rapunzel lowers her hair.*

WIFE: Excuse me for this.

> *Wife yanks hair three times; each time Rapunzel lets out an increasingly loud scream. On the third yank, the hair falls into Wife's hands; Wife runs away to another part of the woods; Cinderella enters as if pursued; she falls at Wife's feet.*

You do take plenty of spills, don't you?

CINDERELLA (*Recognizing Wife*): It's these slippers. They're not suited for these surroundings. Actually, they're not much suited for dancing, either. (*She sits, taking off shoes*)

WIFE: I'd say those slippers were as pure as gold.

CINDERELLA: Yes. They are all you could wish for in beauty.

WIFE: What I wouldn't give for just one.

CINDERELLA: One is not likely to do you much good. (*She giggles*)

WIFE: Was the Ball just as wonderful as last evening?

CINDERELLA:
Oh, it's still a nice Ball.

WIFE:
Yes—? And—?

CINDERELLA:
And—
They have far too much food.

WIFE:
No, the Prince—

CINDERELLA:
Oh, the Prince . . .

WIFE:
Yes, the Prince!

CINDERELLA:
> If he knew who I really was—

WIFE:
> Oh? Who?

CINDERELLA:
> I'm afraid I was rude.

WIFE:
> Oh? How?

CINDERELLA:
> Now I'm being pursued.

WIFE:
> Yes? And—?

CINDERELLA:
> And I'm not in the mood.
>
> I have no experience with Princes and castles and gowns.

WIFE: Nonsense, every girl dreams—

> *Fanfare in the distance; we hear voices advancing.*

STEWARD (*Off*): Look, sir! Look!
CINDERELLA'S PRINCE (*Off*): Yes, there she is! Move!
CINDERELLA: I must run.

> *Wife grabs a shoe.*

WIFE: And I must have your shoe.
CINDERELLA: Stop that!

> *The two engage in a violent tug-of-war over the shoe. Cinderella wins the battle and desperately runs off; Wife is embarrassed by her own behavior. She straightens herself up as Cinderella's Prince and Steward bound onstage.*

CINDERELLA'S PRINCE: Where did she go?
WIFE (*Bows*): Who?
STEWARD: Don't play the fool, woman!

WIFE: Oh! You mean the beautiful young maiden in the ball gown? She went in that direction. I was trying to hold her here for you . . .

CINDERELLA'S PRINCE: I can capture my own damsel, thank you. (*He begins to go off towards Cinderella*)

WIFE: Yes, sir.

> *Prince and Steward dash offstage. We hear Florinda, Lucinda and Stepmother. They enter, first looking behind them, then looking towards the Prince.*

STEPMOTHER (*To Wife*): Where did he go?

WIFE: Who?

LUCINDA: The Prince, of course!

WIFE: That direction. But you'll never reach them!

FLORINDA: We would have if that mongrel with the cow hadn't molested us.

WIFE: Cow?

> *The stepsisters giggle. Baker runs onstage with Milky-White. They are both out of breath.*

BAKER (*Holding up ear of corn*): Please, let me just compare this color with that of your own.

> *Lucinda and Florinda chortle.*

LUCINDA AND FLORINDA: He wants to compare our hair to corn!

> *The threesome exits laughing hysterically. There is a long moment of silence. Wife and Baker stare at one another.*

BAKER (*Dejected*): I thought you were returning home. (*Angry*) I've had no luck.

WIFE: You've the cow!

BAKER: Yes. I've the cow. We've only two of the four.

WIFE: Three.

BAKER: Two.

WIFE (*Pulls the hair from her pocket*): Three! Compare this to your corn.

> *Baker does so and smiles.*

BAKER: Where did you find it?

WIFE (*False modesty*): I pulled it from a maiden in a tower.

BAKER (*Looking at hair*): Three!

WIFE: And I almost had the fourth, but she got away.

BAKER: We've one entire day left. Surely we can locate the slipper by then.

WIFE: *We*? You mean you'll allow me to stay?

BAKER (*Retreating*): Well . . . perhaps it will take the two of us to get this child.

> *Music.*

WIFE:

> You've changed.
> You're daring.
> You're different in the woods.
> More sure.
> More sharing.
> You're getting us through the woods.
>
> If you could see—
> You're not the man who started,
> And much more open-hearted
> Than I knew
> You to be.

BAKER:

> It takes two.
> I thought one was enough,
> It's not true:
> It takes two of us.
> You came through
> When the journey was rough.
> It took you.
> It took two of us.
>
> It takes care,
> It takes patience and fear and despair
> To change.
> Though you swear
> To change,
> Who can tell if you do?
> It takes two.

WIFE:

> You've changed.
> You're thriving.
> There's something about the woods.
> Not just
> Surviving,
> You're blossoming in the woods.

> At home I'd fear
> We'd stay the same forever.
> And then out here
> You're passionate, charming, considerate, clever—

BAKER:

> It takes one
> To begin, but then once
> You've begun,
> It takes two of you.
> It's no fun,
> But what needs to be done
> You can do
> When there's two of you.

> If I dare,
> It's because I'm becoming
> Aware of us
> As a pair of us,
> Each accepting a share
> Of what's there.

BOTH:

> We've changed.
> We're strangers.
> I'm meeting you in the woods.
> Who minds
> What dangers?
> I know we'll get past the woods.
> And once we're past,
> Let's hope the changes last

> Beyond woods,
> Beyond witches and slippers and hoods,
> Just the two of us—

Beyond lies,
Safe at home with our beautiful prize,
Just the few of us.

It takes trust.
It takes just
A bit more
And we're done.
We want four,
We had none.
We've got three.
We need one.
It takes two.

*We hear the slow chimes of midnight begin; a hen
dashes onstage, closely followed by Jack.*

JACK: STOP HER! STOP THAT HEN!

Baker grabs hen.

Oh, Providence! My Milky-White. (*He gives cow a kiss*)
And the owners. *And* my hen!

BAKER (*Squeals*): Look what this hen has dropped in my hand!

WIFE (*Excited*): A golden egg! I've never seen a golden egg!

JACK: You see, I promised you more than the five gold pieces I
gave you, sir.

WIFE: Five gold pieces?

JACK: Now I'm taking my cow.

WIFE: Five gold pieces?

BAKER (*To Jack*): Now, I never said I would sell.

JACK: But you took the five gold pieces.

WIFE: You took five gold pieces?!

BAKER: I didn't take, you gave.

WIFE: Where are the five gold pieces?

BAKER: An old man—

*Jack goes to take Milky-White. Baker holds her
rope from him. Simultaneous dialogue:*

JACK (*Getting upset*): You said I could have my cow!

BAKER: Now I never said you could. I said you might.

WIFE: You would take money before a child?!

56

Milky-White lets out a terrible moan, and falls to the ground, dead. Silence. Jack runs to her, puts his ear to her chest. Silence.

JACK: Milky-White is dead . . .
BAKER, WIFE (*Exasperated*): Two!

Last chime of midnight; blackout.

Scene 4

Again, the characters appear one by one, as night changes into dawn.

WITCH:
Two midnights gone!

CINDERELLA:
Wanting a ball is not wanting a Prince . . .

CINDERELLA'S PRINCE:
Near may be better than far,
But it still isn't *there* . . .

RAPUNZEL'S PRINCE:
Near may be better than far,
But it still isn't *there* . . .

CINDERELLA:
The ball . . .

CINDERELLA'S PRINCE:
So near . . .

RAPUNZEL'S PRINCE:
So far . . .

STEPMOTHER:
You can never love somebody else's child—

FLORINDA, LUCINDA:
Two midnights gone!

STEPMOTHER:
    —the way you love—

CINDERELLA'S PRINCE:
    So near . . .

STEPMOTHER:
    —your own.

CINDERELLA:
    The Prince . . .

RAPUNZEL'S PRINCE:
    So far . . .

GRANNY:
    The greatest prize can often lie
    At the end of the thorniest path . . .

ALL:

    Two midnights gone!
    Two midnights gone!

Scene 5

*As the lights come up, we see the Wife and the
Baker, bedraggled and exhausted.*

NARRATOR: Two midnights gone. And the exhausted baker and
    his wife buried the dead Milky-White, believing that
    when the witch said a cow as white as milk, she was
    referring to a live one.
BAKER: You must go to the village in search of another cow.
WIFE: And what do you propose I use to purchase this cow?
BAKER (*Takes remaining bean from pocket*): Here. Tell them it's
    magic.
WIFE: No person with a brain larger than this is going to
    exchange a cow for a bean.
BAKER (*Losing patience*): Then steal it.
WIFE (*Angry*): Steal it? Just two days ago *you* were accusing *me*
    of exercising deceit in securing the cow.

BAKER: Then don't steal it and resign yourself to a childless life.

WIFE (*Calm, but cold*): I feel it best you go for the cow, as I have met a maiden with a golden slipper these previous eves, and I think I might succeed in winning one of her shoes.

BAKER: Fine. That is simply fine.

Wife gathers her things and begins to exit in one direction, the Baker in the other; we hear Rapunzel scream; they run off in fear.

NARRATOR: Unfortunately for Rapunzel—

RAPUNZEL (*Off*): No!

NARRATOR: —the witch discovered her affections for the Prince before he could spirit her away.

Witch drags Rapunzel on. Music.

WITCH:

What did I clearly say?
Children must listen.
  (*Grabs Rapunzel's hair, takes out scissors*)

RAPUNZEL:

No, no, please!

WITCH:

What were you not to do?
Children must see—

RAPUNZEL:

No!

WITCH:

And learn.

Rapunzel screams in protest.

Why could you not obey?
Children should listen.
What have I been to you?
What would you have me be?
Handsome like a Prince?

Rapunzel whimpers.

Ah, but I am old.
I am ugly.
I embarrass you.

RAPUNZEL:

No!

WITCH:

You are ashamed of me.

RAPUNZEL:

No!

WITCH:

You are ashamed.
You don't understand.

Music continues under.

RAPUNZEL: It was lonely atop that tower.
WITCH: I was not company enough?
RAPUNZEL: I am no longer a child. I wish to see the world.
WITCH (*Tender but intense*):

Don't you know what's out there in the world?
Someone has to shield you from the world.
Stay with me.

Princes wait there in the world, it's true.
Princes, yes, but wolves and humans, too.
Stay at home.
I am home.

Who out there could love you more than I?
What out there that I cannot supply?
Stay with me.

Stay with me,
The world is dark and wild.
Stay a child while you can be a child.
With me.

Rapunzel just whimpers; music continues under.

I gave you protection and yet you disobeyed me.
RAPUNZEL: No!
WITCH: Why didn't you tell me you had a visitor?

Rapunzel keeps whimpering; music crescendos.

I will not share you, but I *will* show you a world you've never seen. (*She cuts Rapunzel's hair*)
RAPUNZEL: No! NO!

Witch drags Rapunzel off. Baker enters, followed by Mysterious Man.

MYSTERIOUS MAN: When is a white cow not a white cow?
BAKER: I don't know! Leave me alone!
MYSTERIOUS MAN: Haven't I left you alone long enough?
BAKER: Your questions make no sense, old man! Go away!
MYSTERIOUS MAN: In need of another cow?

He drops sack of gold; Baker turns around at the sound of the falling coins; Mysterious Man exits as Baker picks up money and exits. Jack comes upon Little Red Ridinghood, who wears a cape made of wolfskins. She walks with a certain bravado.

JACK: What a beautiful cape!

Little Red Ridinghood swerves around, brandishing a knife.

LITTLE RED RIDINGHOOD: Stay away from my cape or I'll slice you into a thousand bits!
JACK (*Stepping back*): I don't want it! I was just admiring it!
LITTLE RED RIDINGHOOD (*Proud*): My granny made it for me from a wolf that attacked us. And I got to skin the animal—and best of all, she gave me this beautiful knife for protection.
JACK (*Competitive*): Well, look what *I* have. A hen that lays golden eggs.
LITTLE RED RIDINGHOOD (*Suspicious*): I don't believe that egg came from that hen. Where did you get that egg?
JACK: I stole this from the kingdom of the giant—up there. And if you think this is something, you should see the golden harp the giant has. It plays the most beautiful tunes without your even having to touch it.
LITTLE RED RIDINGHOOD (*Smirking*): Of course it does. Why don't you go up to the kingdom right now and bring it back and show me?

JACK: I could.

LITTLE RED RIDINGHOOD: You could not!

JACK: I could!

LITTLE RED RIDINGHOOD: You could not, Mr. *Liar*! (*She makes a hasty exit*)

JACK: I am not a liar! I'll get that harp. You'll see! (*He exits*)

NARRATOR: After having cast out Rapunzel to a remote desert, the witch returned to take the Prince by surprise.

> *Rapunzel's tower. Rapunzel's Prince climbs Rapunzel's hair when suddenly the Witch pops out from the tower.*

WITCH: You would fetch your dearest, but the bird no longer sits in her cage.

> *The Witch pushes Rapunzel's Prince from the tower. He falls and screams, grabbing his eyes. The Witch laughs with delight.*

NARRATOR: And unfortunately, the Prince fell into a patch of thorns which pierced his eyes and blinded him.

> *Rapunzel's Prince stumbles helplessly offstage.*

As for Cinderella, she returned from her final visit to the Festival.

> *Lights dim. Cinderella hobbles onstage, wearing but one shoe.*

CINDERELLA:

> He's a very smart Prince,
> He's a Prince who prepares.
> Knowing this time I'd run from him,
> He spread pitch on the stairs.
> I was caught unawares.
>
> And I thought: well, he cares—
> This is more than just malice.
> Better stop and take stock
> While you're standing here stuck
> On the steps of the palace.
>
> You think, what do you want?
> You think, make a decision.

Why not stay and be caught?
You think, well, it's a thought,
What would be his response?
But then what if he knew
Who you were when you know
That you're not what he thinks
That he wants?

And then what if you are
What a Prince would envision?
Although how can you know
Who you are till you know
What you want, which you don't?
So then which do you pick:
Where you're safe, out of sight,
And yourself, but where everything's wrong?
Or where everything's right
And you know that you'll never belong?

And whichever you pick,
Do it quick,
'Cause you're starting to stick
To the steps of the palace.

It's your first big decision,
The choice isn't easy to make.
To arrive at a Ball
Is exciting and all—
Once you're there, though, it's scary.
And it's fun to deceive
When you know you can leave,
But you have to be wary.

There's a lot that's at stake,
But you've stalled long enough
'Cause you're still standing stuck
In the stuff on the steps . . .

Better run along home
And avoid the collision.
Even though they don't care,
You'll be better off there

Where there's nothing to choose,
So there's nothing to lose.

So you pry up your shoes.

Then from out of the blue,
And without any guide,
You know what your decision is,
Which is not to decide.

You'll just leave him a clue:
For example, a shoe.
And then see what he'll do.

Now it's he and not you
Who is stuck with a shoe,
In a stew,
In the goo,
And you've learned something, too,
Something you never knew,
On the steps of the palace.

Wife races onstage.

CINDERELLA: Don't come any closer to me!
WIFE (*Breathless*): Please, just hear me out!
CINDERELLA: We have nothing to discuss. You have attacked me once before—
WIFE: I did not attack *you*! I attacked your shoe. I need it.

Cinderella begins to run away; Wife reaches into her pocket.

Here. Here is a magic bean in exchange for it.

Cinderella stops; Wife hands her the bean.

CINDERELLA: Magic bean? (*Takes bean, looks at it*) Nonsense! (*Throws the bean away*)
WIFE: Don't do that! (*Drops to the ground and searches for it*)
CINDERELLA: I've already given up one shoe this evening. My feet cannot bear to give up another. (*Begins to leave*)
WIFE (*Rising, desperate*): I need that shoe to have a child!
CINDERELLA: That makes no sense!

We hear rumblings from the distance.

WIFE: Does it make sense that you're running from a Prince?
STEWARD (*Off*): Stop!
WIFE: Here. Take my shoes. You'll run faster.

> *Wife gives Cinderella her shoes, and takes the golden slipper. Cinderella exits. Steward bounds onstage; looks about.*

STEWARD: Who was that woman?
WIFE: I do not know, sir.
STEWARD: Lying will cost you your life!

> *Baker enters with another cow.*

WIFE: I've done nothing . . .
BAKER: I've the cow.
WIFE (*Sees the cow; excitedly to Baker*): The slipper! We've all four! (*She runs to the Baker*)
STEWARD (*Goes to Wife and takes the shoe*): I will give this to the Prince and we will search the kingdom tomorrow for the maiden who will fit this shoe.
WIFE (*Tries to grab the slipper back*): It's mine!

> *They begin to struggle; Mysterious Man comes from around a tree.*

I don't care if this costs me my life—
MYSTERIOUS MAN (*Simultaneously*): Give her the slipper and all will—

> *Suddenly there is a long sound of crackling wood, followed by an enormous thud. This noise is frighteningly loud: very bass, with the kind of reverberation that will shake the audience. All action on stage stops. There is a moment of stunned silence. Cinderella's Prince races onstage.*

CINDERELLA'S PRINCE: What was that noise?
STEWARD: Sir. Just a bolt of lightning in a far-off kingdom.
CINDERELLA'S PRINCE (*To Steward*): How dare you go off in search without me!
STEWARD: My apologies, sir. I thought that I might—
CINDERELLA'S PRINCE: Enough of what you thought! I employed a ruse and had the entire staircase smeared with

pitch. And there, when she ran down, remained the maiden's slipper. (*He produces the slipper*)

STEWARD: Brilliant!

CINDERELLA'S PRINCE: I thought so. It did create quite a mess when the other guests left.

STEWARD: And sir, I have succeeded in obtaining the other slipper!

MYSTERIOUS MAN (*To Steward*): Give them the slipper, and all will come to a happy end.

STEWARD: Who are you, old man?

MYSTERIOUS MAN: When first I appear, I seem deleterious—

STEWARD: Shut up!

CINDERELLA'S PRINCE: Do as he says. He's obviously a spirit of some sort, and we only need one.

STEWARD: Oh . . .

He hands slipper back to Wife. Loud scream. Jack's Mother comes running onstage, still screaming.

JACK'S MOTHER (*Hysterical; she bows*): There's a dead giant in my backyard!

Cinderella's Prince shoots Steward a look.

(*More hysterical*) I heard Jack coming down the beanstalk, calling for his axe. And when he raced to the bottom he took it and began hacking down the stalk. Suddenly, with a crash, the beanstalk fell, but there was no Jack. For all I know, he's been crushed by the ogre.

She cries; long pause; Cinderella's Prince goes to her.

CINDERELLA'S PRINCE: Worrying will do you no good. If he's safe, then he's safe. If he's been crushed, well, then, there's nothing any of us can do about that, now is there? (*To Steward*) We must be off. I need my rest before tomorrow's search is to commence.

Prince and Steward begin to exit.

JACK'S MOTHER: Doesn't anyone care a giant has fallen from the sky?

CINDERELLA'S PRINCE (*Stops*): He is dead, isn't he?
JACK'S MOTHER: With such a thud, I would suppose.

> *Cinderella's Prince nods, and exits with Steward.*
> *Witch appears, frantic; looks up to the sky.*

WITCH (*Unpleasant*): The third midnight is near. I see a cow. I see a slipper.
BAKER (*Pulling items from his bag*): And the cape as red as blood.
WIFE: And the hair as yellow as corn.
WITCH (*Amazed*): You've all the objects?
WIFE: Yes. (*She brings the cow forth*)
WITCH: That cow doesn't look as white as milk to me.
WIFE (*Moving towards cow*): Oh, she is. (*Patting cow*) She is!

> *White powder flies about as Wife pats the cow.*
> *Baker pulls her away as Witch approaches.*

WITCH: This cow has been covered with flour!
BAKER: We had a cow as white as milk. Honestly we did.
WITCH: Then where is she?
WIFE: She's dead.
BAKER: We thought you'd prefer a live cow.
WITCH: Of course I'd prefer a live cow! So bring me the dead cow and I'll bring her back to life!
BAKER: You could do that?
WITCH: Now!

> *Witch zaps Baker with lightning; Witch, Wife and Baker scamper upstage towards Milky-White's grave and we see dirt flying into the air as they dig into the grave; Jack comes running onstage with a golden harp that sings.*

JACK'S MOTHER (*Relieved*): There you are! (*She hits him*) I've been worried sick.
JACK: Mother, look. The most beautiful harp. (*He hands harp to her*)
JACK'S MOTHER: You've stolen too much! You could have been killed coming down that plant.
BAKER (*Off*): She's too heavy.
JACK: What's happening?

JACK'S MOTHER: Milky-White is dead, but don't worry. They're going to bring her back to life!

Witch waves her hand, causing a puff of smoke. Milky-White suddenly stands, restored to life. Baker and Wife bring the cow forward.

JACK: Milky-White! Now I have two friends. A cow and a harp.

WITCH: Quiet! Feed the objects to the cow!

JACK, WIFE, BAKER: What?

WITCH: You heard me. Feed them to the cow.

Music; the Baker begins to feed Milky-White the objects. With great effort, the cow chews them and with greater effort, swallows. We hear the first chime of midnight. The remaining eleven sound through the rest of the scene. All stare intently at the cow. The Witch pulls a silver goblet from her cloak and gives it to the Baker.

Fill this!

JACK (*Going to Milky-White*): I'll do it. She'll milk only for me. Squeeze, pal.

Jack milks her feverishly. Nothing. Witch goes and takes the goblet back; she turns it upside down.

WITCH: Wrong ingredients. Forget about a child.

WIFE: Wait! We followed your instructions. One, the cow is as white as milk, correct?

WITCH: Yes.

WIFE: And two, the cape was certainly as red as blood.

WITCH: Yes.

WIFE: And three, the slipper—

WITCH: Yes.

BAKER: And four, I compared the hair with this ear of corn.

WIFE: I pulled it from a maiden in a tower and—

WITCH: YOU WHAT?! What were *you* doing there?

WIFE: Well, I happened to be passing by—

WITCH: I touched that hair! Don't you understand? I cannot have touched the ingredients!

BAKER, WIFE (*Moaning*): Nooooo . . .

Mysterious Man comes from around a tree.

MYSTERIOUS MAN: The corn! The corn!
BAKER: What?
MYSTERIOUS MAN: The silky hair of the corn. Pull it from the ear and feed it to the cow. Quickly!

Baker does so, hurriedly.

WITCH: This had better work, old man, before the last stroke of midnight, or your son will be the last of your flesh and blood.
BAKER: Son?
MYSTERIOUS MAN (*To Witch*): Please. Not now.
WITCH: Yes. Meet your father. (*She moves to cow*)
BAKER: FATHER? Could that be you? I thought you died in a baking accident.
MYSTERIOUS MAN: I didn't want to run away from you, son, but—

Cow lets out a bloodcurdling moan and begins to shake feverishly.

WIFE: It's working!

Cow squeals.

JACK: She's milking!
BAKER (*To Mysterious Man*): I don't understand.
MYSTERIOUS MAN: Not now! (*To Wife*) Into the cup!

Wife holds goblet under cow's udder as Jack milks; all eyes are on the cow. Wife hands the filled goblet to the Witch; Baker and Wife dance with joy as Witch drinks potion. They go to her.

BAKER: We've given you what you wish.
WIFE: Now when can we expect a child?

Witch begins to shake and move away.

BAKER: What's wrong? What's happening?
WIFE: Wait. Where are you going?

The last stroke of midnight.

MYSTERIOUS MAN (*Falling to the ground*): Son! Son!
BAKER (*Going to Mysterious Man's side*): Father!

> *Mysterious Man lets out a groan.*

MYSTERIOUS MAN: All is repaired. (*He dies*)
BAKER: He's dead!

> *The Witch with a flourish turns around. She has been transformed into a beautiful woman. Blackout.*

Scene 6

> *Music under; the Mysterious Man removes elements of his costume, revealing that he is also the Narrator. He tosses the Mysterious Man's clothing away.*

NARRATOR: And so the mysterious man died, having helped end the curse on his house. For the baker, there would be no reunion with his father, and he and his wife, bewildered, returned home. The witch, who had been punished with age and ugliness that night when her beans had been stolen and the lightning flashed, was now returned to her former state of youth and beauty. And Milky-White, after a night of severe indigestion, was reunited with the now wealthy Jack. As for the Prince, he began his search for the foot to fit the golden slipper.

> *Fanfare; Cinderella's Prince and Steward enter on horseback.*

When he came to Cinderella's house, Cinderella's stepmother took the slipper into Florinda's room.

> *Florinda tries on shoe; Stepmother struggles to help her.*

FLORINDA:
> Careful, my toe—!

STEPMOTHER:
> Darling, I know—

FLORINDA:
> What'll we do?

STEPMOTHER:
> It'll have to go—

> *Florinda reacts as Stepmother suddenly brandishes a knife.*

> But when you're his bride
> You can sit or ride.
> You'll never need to walk!

> *Stepmother looks at her encouragingly and cuts off toe.*

NARRATOR: The girl obeyed, swallowing the pain, and joined the Prince on his horse, riding off to become his bride.

> *Prince puts Florinda on the back of his horse; they arrive at the grave of Cinderella's Mother; birds cry from the tree.*

CINDERELLA'S MOTHER:
> Look at the blood within the shoe;
> This one is not the bride that's true.
> Search for the foot that fits.

> *Prince looks at Florinda's foot and sees blood trickling from the shoe. They return to Cinderella's home.*

NARRATOR: The Prince returned the false bride, and asked the other sister to put on the shoe.

> *Stepmother tries forcing shoe onto Lucinda's foot.*

LUCINDA:
> Why won't it fit?

STEPMOTHER (*Holding the knife*):
> Darling, be still.
> Cut off a bit
> Of the heel and it will.
> And when you're his wife

You'll have such a life,
You'll never need to walk!

Stepmother looks at her encouragingly and cuts off heel.

NARRATOR: The girl obeyed and swallowed her pain. But as she was helped on the back of the horse by the Prince, he noticed blood trickling from the shoe.

Prince takes shoe off, pours blood from it and, ashen, returns it to Stepmother.

CINDERELLA'S PRINCE: Have you no other daughters?
NARRATOR: To which the woman replied:
STEPMOTHER: No, only a little stunted kitchen wench which his late wife left behind, but she is much too dirty; she cannot present herself.
CINDERELLA'S PRINCE: I insist.

Cinderella appears.

NARRATOR: And when Cinderella presented herself and tried on the blood-soaked slipper, it fit like a glove.
CINDERELLA'S PRINCE: This is the true bride!
CINDERELLA'S FATHER: I always wanted a son!

Cinderella's Father is admonished by Stepmother and stepsisters; fanfare.

NARRATOR: And much to the dismay of the stepmother and her daughters, he took Cinderella on his horse and rode off.

Cinderella's Prince and Cinderella ride up to the grave.

CINDERELLA'S MOTHER:
No blood at all within the shoe;
This is the proper bride for you,
Fit to attend a Prince.

Rapunzel, with babies, enters. Rapunzel's Prince falls into her arms; his sight is restored.

NARRATOR: And finally, as for Rapunzel, she bore twins, and lived impoverished in the desert until the day her

Sondheim & Lapine

Prince, wandering aimlessly, heard a voice so familiar that he went towards it. And when he approached, Rapunzel, overjoyed at seeing him, fell into his arms, weeping. Two of her tears wetted his eyes and their touch restored his vision.

Witch enters.

WITCH (*To Rapunzel*): I was going to come fetch you as soon as you learned your lesson.

RAPUNZEL: Who are you?

WITCH: Surely you remember.

RAPUNZEL: Mother?

WITCH: This is who I truly am. Come with me, child. We can be happy as we once were. (*She offers Rapunzel her hand*)

RAPUNZEL'S PRINCE (*Pulling Rapunzel back*): She will not go with you!

WITCH: Let her speak for herself!

Rapunzel shakes her head ''no.''

You are the only family I know. (*Holds out her hand*) Come with me. Please.

Rapunzel shakes her head ''no.''

You give me no choice!

Witch goes to put a spell on them, but only a pathetic puff of smoke comes from her hand; she tries again. No success. The couple, bewildered, exit.

NARRATOR: As is often the way in these tales, in exchange for her youth and beauty, the witch lost her power.

Witch, frustrated, breaks her cane and exits.

When the wedding with the Prince was celebrated, Lucinda and Florinda attended, wishing to win favor with Cinderella and share her good fortune.

Cinderella, in her wedding gown, and Cinderella's Prince enter with Stepmother, Cinderella's Father, Lucinda and Florinda.

73

But as the sisters stood by the blessed couple, pigeons swooped down upon them and poked out their eyes and punished them with blindness.

Florinda and Lucinda are blinded by birds and stagger offstage, screaming; Wife, very pregnant, enters.

WIFE: I see your Prince has found you.

CINDERELLA: Yes.

WIFE (*Patting her belly*): Thank you for the slipper.

Baker enters.

CINDERELLA:
   I didn't think I'd wed a Prince.

CINDERELLA'S PRINCE:
   I didn't think I'd ever find you.

CINDERELLA, CINDERELLA'S PRINCE, BAKER, WIFE:
   I didn't think I could be so happy! . . .

The company comes onstage; segue to Finale music.

NARRATOR: And it came to pass, all that seemed wrong was now right, the kingdoms were filled with joy, and those who deserved to were certain to live a long and happy life. Ever after . . .

COMPANY:
   Ever after!

NARRATOR:
   Journey over, all is mended,
   And it's not just for today,
   But tomorrow, and extended
   Ever after!

COMPANY:
   Ever after!

NARRATOR:
   All the curses have been ended,
   The reverses wiped away.

All is tenderness and laughter
For forever after!

COMPANY:

Happy now and happy hence
And happy ever after!

NARRATOR:

There were dangers—

COMPANY:

We were frightened—

NARRATOR:

And confusions—

COMPANY:

But we hid it—

NARRATOR:

And the paths would often swerve.

COMPANY:

We did not.

NARRATOR:

There were constant—

COMPANY:

It's amazing—

NARRATOR:

Disillusions—

COMPANY:

That we did it.

NARRATOR:

But they never lost their nerve.

COMPANY:

Not a lot.

NARRATOR, COMPANY:

And they (we) reached the right conclusions,
And they (we) got what they (we) deserve!

COMPANY:
> Not a sigh and not a sorrow,
> Tenderness and laughter.
> Joy today and bliss tomorrow,
> And forever after!

FLORINDA:
> I was greedy.

LUCINDA:
> I was vain.

FLORINDA:
> I was haughty.

LUCINDA:
> I was smug.

BOTH:
> We were happy.

LUCINDA:
> It was fun.

FLORINDA:
> But we were blind.

BOTH:
> Then we went into the woods
> To get our wish
> And now we're really blind.

WITCH (*Overlapping*):
> I was perfect.
> I had everything but beauty.
> I had power,
> And a daughter like a flower,
> In a tower.
> Then I went into the woods
> To get my wish
> And now I'm ordinary.
> Lost my power, and my flower.

FLORINDA, LUCINDA:
> We're unworthy.

FLORINDA, LUCINDA, WITCH:
> We're (I'm) unhappy now, unhappy hence,
> As well as ever after.
> Had we used our common sense,
> Been worthy of our discontents . . .

COMPANY:
> To be happy, and forever,
> You must see your wish come true.
> Don't be careful, don't be clever.
> When you see your wish, pursue.
> It's a dangerous endeavor,
> But the only thing to do—
>
> *(In three groups)*
> Though it's fearful,
> Though it's deep, though it's dark,
> And though you may lose the path,
> Though you may encounter wolves,
> You mustn't stop,
> You mustn't swerve,
> You mustn't ponder,
> You have to act!
> When you know your wish,
> If you want your wish,
> You can have your wish,
> But you can't just wish—
> No, to get your wish
>
> *(In unison)*
> You go into the woods,
> Where nothing's clear,
> Where witches, ghosts
> And wolves appear.
> Into the woods
> And through the fear,
> You have to take the journey.
>
> Into the woods
> And down the dell,
> In vain perhaps,
> But who can tell?

Into the woods to lift the spell,
Into the woods to lose the longing.
Into the woods to have the child,
To wed the Prince,
To get the money,
To save the house,
To kill the wolf,
To find the father,
To conquer the kingdom,
To have, to wed,
To get, to save,
To kill, to keep,
To go to the Festival!

Into the woods,
Into the woods,
Into the woods,
Then out of the woods—

NARRATOR: To be continued . . .

A giant beanstalk emerges from the ground and stretches to the heavens; the characters are oblivious to its presence.

ALL:

—and happy ever after!

The parties head off to their respective homes, as the lights dim to black.

INTERMISSION

ACT TWO

Above: Anna Kendrick as Cinderella

Below: Lucy Punch, Christine Baranski and Tammy Blanchard
as Cinderella's evil stepsisters and stepmother

Overleaf: Lilla Crawford as Little Red Ridinghood

(Photos by Peter Mountain)

Above: Chris Pine as Cinderella's prince
Below: Daniel Huttlestone as Jack and Tracey Ullman as his mother

Above: James Corden as the baker, Emily Blunt as his wife and Meryl Streep as the witch

Below: Billy Magnussen as Rapunzel's prince

Overleaf: James Corden and Meryl Streep

MacKenzie Mauzy as Rapunzel

Scene 1

Downstage, three structures:
Far left, the castle where Cinderella now lives. She
sits on her throne, as Florinda and Lucinda, both
still blind, attend to her. The Stepmother super-
vises.
Center, the cottage where Jack lives, now dramat-
ically improved. He and his Mother are inside,
along with Milky-White and the golden harp.
Far right, the home/workplace of the Baker and his
Wife. It is very cluttered with both baking supplies
and nursery items. Wife holds their baby, who
does not stop crying.
Behind these homes the backdrop of the forest re-
mains.
Narrator steps forward.

NARRATOR: Once upon a time—

Music.

—later—

Light on Cinderella.

CINDERELLA:
   I wish . . .

NARRATOR: —in the same far-off kingdom—
CINDERELLA:
   More than anything . . .

NARRATOR: —lived a young Princess—
CINDERELLA:
   More than life . . .

NARRATOR: —the lad Jack—

Light on Jack.

CINDERELLA:
   More than footmen . . .

JACK:
   I wish . . .

NARRATOR: —and the baker and his family—

Light on the Baker and his Wife with their baby.

BABY:
> Waaah!

JACK:
> No, I miss . . .

CINDERELLA, BAKER:
> I wish . . .

BABY:
> Waaah!

JACK:
> More than anything . . .

CINDERELLA, BAKER, JACK:
> More than the moon . . .

WIFE (*To the baby*): There, there . . .
CINDERELLA:
> I wish to sponsor a Festival.

BABY:
> Waaah!

BAKER:
> More than life . . .

JACK:
> I miss . . .

CINDERELLA:
> The time has come for a Festival . . .

BABY:
> Waaah!

WIFE: Shh . . .
BAKER (*Overlapping*):
> More than riches . . .

CINDERELLA:
> And a Ball . . .

JACK:
> I miss my kingdom up in the sky.

CINDERELLA, BAKER:
> More than anything . . .

WIFE:
> I wish we had more room . . .

JACK (*To harp*):
> Play, harp . . .

BAKER:
> Another room . . .

Jack strums the harp, and it sings.

NARRATOR: But despite some minor inconveniences, they were all content . . .

Cinderella's Prince enters castle.

CINDERELLA:
> I never thought I'd wed a Prince . . .

CINDERELLA'S PRINCE:
> I never thought I'd find perfection . . .

BOTH:
> I never thought I could be so happy!

CINDERELLA:
> Not an unhappy moment since . . .

JACK, JACK'S MOTHER:
> I didn't think we'd be this rich . . .

CINDERELLA'S PRINCE:
> Not a conceivable objection . . .

BAKER, WIFE:
> I never thought we'd have a baby . . .

CINDERELLA, CINDERELLA'S PRINCE, JACK, JACK'S MOTHER:
> I never thought I could be so happy!

BAKER, WIFE (*Overlapping*):
> I'm so happy!

STEPMOTHER:
>Happy now,
>Happy hence,
>Happy ever after—

STEPMOTHER, STEPSISTERS (*To Cinderella*):
>We're so happy you're so happy!
>Just as long as you stay happy,
>We'll stay happy! . . .

CINDERELLA, CINDERELLA'S PRINCE:
>Not one row . . .

JACK'S MOTHER:
>Pots of pence . . .

JACK:
>With my cow . . .

BAKER, WIFE:
>Little gurgles . . .

CINDERELLA'S PRINCE (*To Cinderella*):
>Darling, I must go now . . . (*Exits*)

JACK'S MOTHER (*To Jack*):
>We should really sell it.

BAKER (*To Wife*):
>Where's the cheesecloth?

ALL OTHERS:
>Wishes may bring problems,
>Such that you regret them.

ALL:
>Better that, though,
>Than to never get them . . .

CINDERELLA:
>I'm going to be a perfect wife!

JACK (*Overlapping*):
>I'm going to be a perfect son!

WIFE, JACK'S MOTHER:
>I'm going to be a perfect mother!

BAKER:
> I'm going to be a perfect father!
> I'm so happy!

CINDERELLA, JACK, JACK'S MOTHER, WIFE:
> I'm going to see that he (she)
> Is so happy!

ALL:
> I never thought I'd love my life!
> I would have settled for another!

CINDERELLA:
> Then to become a wife . . .

JACK, JACK'S MOTHER:
> Then to be set for life . . .

BAKER, WIFE:
> Then to beget a child . . .

ALL:
> That fortune smiled . . .
> I'm so happy.

Music continues under.

WIFE (*Handing the baby to the Baker, who is very awkward holding the child*): If only this cottage were a little larger.
BAKER: I will expand our quarters in due time.
WIFE: Why expand when we could simply move to another cottage?

Baby cries.

BAKER: We will not move. This was my father's house, and now it will be my son's.
WIFE: You would raise your child alongside a witch?
BAKER (*Edgy*): Why does he always cry when I hold him.
WIFE: Babies cry. He's fine. You needn't hold him as if he were so fragile.
BAKER: He wants his mother. Here.

Baker carefully passes baby back to his Wife; baby stops crying.

WIFE: I can't take care of him all of the time!

BAKER: I will care for him . . . when he's older.

BAKER, WIFE, JACK, JACK'S MOTHER:
We had to go through thick and thin.

STEPMOTHER, LUCINDA, FLORINDA:
We had to lose a lot to win.

CINDERELLA:
I ventured out and saw within.

ALL:
I never thought I'd be so much I hadn't been!
I'm so hap—

The song is interrupted by a loud rumbling noise followed by an enormous crash. The Baker's house caves in. He is caught underneath the rubble as the Wife runs forward with their baby. Action stops onstage. Jack and his Mother look concerned. Cinderella sends her Stepmother out to investigate. We should be momentarily uncertain as to whether there has truly been an accident onstage.

BAKER (*Stunned*): Are you all right?

WIFE: I think so.

BAKER: And the baby?

WIFE: Yes, he's fine. And you?

He nods; Witch races in; she is disheveled. Music under.

BAKER: YOU! Have you done this to our house?

WITCH: Always thinking of yourself! Look at my garden.

WIFE: What of your garden?

WITCH: Look!

Baker and Wife move to window.

BAKER: Destroyed.

WIFE: What has happened?

WITCH: I was thrown to the ground. I saw nothing.

WIFE: What could do such a thing?

BAKER: An earthquake.

WITCH: No earthquake! My garden has been trampled. Those
    are footprints!

WIFE: Who could do such a thing?

WITCH: Anything that leaves a footprint that large is no
    "who."

BAKER:
    Do you think it was a bear?

WITCH:
    A bear? Bears are sweet.
    Besides, you ever see a bear with forty-foot feet?

WIFE:
    Dragon?

WITCH (*Shakes her head*):
    No scorch marks—
    Usually they're linked.

BAKER:
    Manticore?

WITCH:
    Imaginary.

WIFE, BAKER:
    Griffin?

WITCH:
    Extinct.

BAKER:
    Giant?

WITCH:
    Possible.
    Very, very possible . . .

    Music fades under.

BAKER: A giant . . .

WIFE: Maybe we should tell someone.

WITCH: Who are you going to tell?

BAKER: The royal family, of course.

WITCH (*Lets out a loud cackle*): I wouldn't count on that family to
    snuff out a rat! With a giant, we'll all have to go to

battle! (*Change of tone*) A giant's the worst! A giant has a brain. Hard to outwit a giant. A giant's just like us— only bigger! Much, much bigger! (*She sees a bug crawling across the floor*) So big that we are just an expendable bug beneath its foot. (*She steps on the bug*) BOOM CRUNCH!

We hear the bug crunch as she grinds it into the floor; she then picks it up and eats it; she exits.

WIFE: We are moving!

NARRATOR: And so, the baker proceeded to the castle, but not before visiting Jack and his mother.

Music continues; knock on Jack's door; Baker enters.

JACK: Look, Milky-White. It's the butcher.

BAKER: The baker.

JACK: The baker . . .

JACK'S MOTHER (*Pushing Jack out of the way*): What can we do for you, sir?

BAKER: I'm here to investigate the destruction that was wrought upon our house today.

JACK'S MOTHER (*Defensive*): Jack has been home with me all day.

NARRATOR: The baker told Jack and his mother that he feared there was a giant in the land.

JACK: I can recognize a giant's footstep! I could go to your house—

JACK'S MOTHER: You'll do no such thing!

BAKER: Any help at all—

JACK'S MOTHER: I am sorry, but you'll get none from us. (*She opens the door for the Baker*) No one cared when there was a giant in my backyard! I don't remember *you* volunteering to come to my aid.

BAKER: A giant in your backyard is one thing. A crushed home is quite another.

JACK'S MOTHER (*Change of tone*): Look, young man. Giants never strike the same house twice. I wouldn't worry.

BAKER: I am taking the news to the castle, nonetheless. (*He exits*)

NARRATOR: When the baker reached the castle, it was the Princess who greeted his news. The story unfolds.

Fanfare; Steward enters.

STEWARD: Excuse me, madame. This small man insists on seeing you.

Baker enters.

BAKER: Princess, I've come to report the appearance of a giant in the land.
CINDERELLA: Where did you see a giant?
BAKER: Well, I didn't exactly see it.
STEWARD: Then how do you know there is a giant in the land?
BAKER: Our house was destroyed and there are footprints—
STEWARD: That could have been caused by any number of things. I will show you to the door.
CINDERELLA: Wait.
BAKER: A nearby household was visited by a giant not long ago . . . descending from a beanstalk—
CINDERELLA: Yes, I remember.
STEWARD: That giant was slain. Now come along—
BAKER (*Apologetic*): Wait, please. We have a young child! Princess, our child was very difficult to come by. His safety is of great importance to me.
STEWARD: Are we entirely through now?
BAKER: Yes.
CINDERELLA: I will take this news up with the Prince when he returns. Thank you.

Baker and Steward exit.

JACK'S MOTHER (*With her coat on*): I'm going off to market, Jack.
JACK: Goodbye, Mother.
JACK'S MOTHER: Now, I want you to stay inside.
JACK: But I haven't been outside all day!
JACK'S MOTHER: Jack. Listen to me! I don't want you out when there might be a giant on the loose.
JACK: But I know how to kill a giant!
JACK'S MOTHER: Please! We've had our fill of giants.
JACK: But Mother, if I could help—
JACK'S MOTHER: Enough! Promise me, son, you won't leave your surroundings.
JACK: But Mother, I'm a man now.

JACK'S MOTHER: You're still a little boy in your mother's eyes. I want you to promise. (*Pause; she smacks him*) Promise!

JACK (*Humiliated*): I promise.

> *Jack's Mother gives him a peck on the cheek, exits. Little Red Ridinghood knocks on the Baker's door and enters.*

LITTLE RED RIDINGHOOD: What happened to your house?

WIFE: We've had a baking accident.

BAKER: Baking accident?

WIFE (*Whispers to him*): No use frightening the young thing.

BAKER (*Whispers back*): You can't frighten *her.*

LITTLE RED RIDINGHOOD: Well, I guess Granny will have to do without the bread and sweets. Besides, I have all I can carry.

WIFE: Why such a load?

LITTLE RED RIDINGHOOD: Oh. I'm moving in with Granny. We had an accident, too. I came home to find our house collapsed. As if a big wind blew it in. I couldn't find my mother anywhere.

WIFE: Oh, no.

LITTLE RED RIDINGHOOD: So I salvaged what I could, and now I'm off.

> *Music continues; birds descend; they chirp to Cinderella.*

CINDERELLA: Oh, good friends. What news have you?

> *She listens.*

What of Mother's grave?

> *She listens.*

What kind of trouble?!

> *She listens.*

Oh, no. I can't investigate. A Princess is not supposed to go into the woods unescorted.

> *She begins to cry; birds chirp.*

Good idea! I will disguise myself and go to see what's wrong. Thank you, birds.

Birds ascend. Cinderella exits.

WIFE: We'll take you to Granny's.
BAKER: What?!
WIFE (*Whispers*): We're not going to let her go alone!
BAKER: All right. I will take you.
LITTLE RED RIDINGHOOD: I don't need anyone to take me. I've gone many times before.
BAKER: But not when there have been such winds blowing.
WIFE: That's right. We'll all take you.
BAKER: No!
WIFE: I'm not about to stay here with the baby when a "wind" might return to this house, too.

> *Cinderella returns, dressed in her dirty attire from Act One.*

JACK: I know Mother made me promise, but I'm going to find that giant anyway!

> *Cinderella, Jack, Baker, Wife and Little Red Ridinghood make their way into the woods; music.*

BAKER:

> Into the woods,
> It's always when
> You think at last
> You're through, and then
> Into the woods you go again
> To take another journey.

WIFE:

> Into the woods,
> The weather's clear,
> We've been before,
> We've nought to fear . . .
> Into the woods, away from here—

JACK:

> Into the woods, to find a giant—!

LITTLE RED RIDINGHOOD:

> Into the woods to Grandmother's house . . .

BAKER:

> Into the woods,
> The path is straight,
> No reason then
> To hesitate—

WIFE:

> Into the woods,
> It's not so late,
> It's just another journey . . .

CINDERELLA:

> Into the woods,
> But not too long:
> The skies are strange,
> The winds are strong.
> Into the woods to see what's wrong . . .

JACK (*Picking up a huge pair of broken eyeglasses*):

> Into the woods to slay the giant!

WIFE:

> Into the woods to shield the child . . .

LITTLE RED RIDINGHOOD:

> To flee the winds . . .

BAKER:

> To find a future . . .

WIFE:

> To shield . . .

JACK:

> To slay . . .

LITTLE RED RIDINGHOOD:

> To flee . . .

BAKER:

> To find . . .

CINDERELLA:

> To fix . . .

WIFE:

> To hide . . .

LITTLE RED RIDINGHOOD:

To move . . .

JACK:

To battle . . .

CINDERELLA:

To see what the trouble is . . .

Music fades.

Scene 2

The woods. Something is wrong. The natural order has been broken. Trees have fallen. The birds no longer chirp.
Rapunzel enters, screaming. The Baker, Wife and Little Red Ridinghood, frightened, run off in one direction, Jack in the other. Rapunzel sits weeping as the Witch appears; music stops.

WITCH (*Urgent*): Rapunzel! What are you doing here?

Rapunzel whimpers.

What's the matter?

RAPUNZEL (*Suddenly laughs*): Oh, nothing! You just locked me in a tower without company for fourteen years, then blinded my Prince and banished me to a desert where I had little to eat, and again no company, and then bore twins! Because of the way *you* treated me, I'll never, *never* be happy! (*She cries*)

WITCH (*Defensive, yet sincere*): I was just trying to be a good mother.

Rapunzel screams and runs off.

Stay with me! There's a giant running about! (*She follows Rapunzel*)

Rapunzel's Prince enters; Cinderella's Prince enters from another direction.

RAPUNZEL'S PRINCE: Good brother! What a surprise.

CINDERELLA'S PRINCE: Brother. How good to see you.

RAPUNZEL'S PRINCE: What brings you into the wood today?

CINDERELLA'S PRINCE: I am investigating news of a giant.

RAPUNZEL'S PRINCE: You? Investigating news of a giant? Father would not even do that! That is business for your steward—or less.

CINDERELLA'S PRINCE (*Defensive*): Well, what brings *you* into the wood?

RAPUNZEL'S PRINCE: My Rapunzel has run off.

CINDERELLA'S PRINCE: Run off?

RAPUNZEL'S PRINCE: She's a changed woman. She has been subject to hysterical fits of crying. Moods that no soul could predict. I know not what to do.

CINDERELLA'S PRINCE: What a pity.

RAPUNZEL'S PRINCE: And Cinderella?

CINDERELLA'S PRINCE: She remains well.

RAPUNZEL'S PRINCE (*Conspiratorial*): Does she? Now, brother. Do tell what you're *really* doing here.

Music.

CINDERELLA'S PRINCE:

> High in a tower—
> Like yours was, but higher—
> A beauty asleep.
> All 'round the tower
> A thicket of briar
> A hundred feet deep.
>
> Agony!
> No frustration more keen,
> When the one thing you want
> Is a thing that you've not even seen.

RAPUNZEL'S PRINCE:

> I've found a casket
> Entirely of glass—
>   (*As Cinderella's Prince starts to protest*)
> No, it's unbreakable.
> Inside—don't ask it—
> A maiden, alas,
> Just as unwakeable—

BOTH:

> What unmistakable agony!
> Is the way always barred?

RAPUNZEL'S PRINCE:

> She has skin white as snow—

CINDERELLA'S PRINCE:

> Did you learn her name?

RAPUNZEL'S PRINCE:

> No,
> There's a dwarf standing guard.

BOTH:

> Agony
> Such that princes must weep!
> Always in thrall most
> To anything almost,
> Or something asleep.

CINDERELLA'S PRINCE:

> If it were not for the thicket—

RAPUNZEL'S PRINCE:

> A thicket's no trick.
> Is it thick?

CINDERELLA'S PRINCE:

> It's the thickest.

RAPUNZEL'S PRINCE:

> The quickest
> Is pick it
> Apart with a stick—

CINDERELLA'S PRINCE:

> Yes, but even one prick—
> It's my thing about blood.

RAPUNZEL'S PRINCE:

> Well, it's sick!

CINDERELLA'S PRINCE:

> It's no sicker
> Than your thing with dwarves.

RAPUNZEL'S PRINCE:
>Dwarfs.

CINDERELLA'S PRINCE:
>Dwarfs . . .

RAPUNZEL'S PRINCE:
>Dwarfs are very upsetting.

BOTH:
>Not forgetting
>The tasks unachievable,
>Mountains unscalable—
>If it's conceivable
>But unavailable,
>Ah-ah-ah-ah-ah-ah-ah-ah-ah-ah-ah-ah—
>
>Agony!

CINDERELLA'S PRINCE:
>Misery!

RAPUNZEL'S PRINCE:
>Woe!

BOTH:
>Not to know what you miss.

CINDERELLA'S PRINCE:
>While they lie there for years—

RAPUNZEL'S PRINCE:
>And you cry on their biers—

BOTH:
>What unbearable bliss!
>Agony
>That can cut like a knife!
>
>Ah, well, back to my wife . . .
>
>*We hear a wail in the distance.*

RAPUNZEL'S PRINCE (*Disappointed*): Rapunzel. I must be off.
Godspeed to you, brother.
CINDERELLA'S PRINCE: Godspeed.

*They exit in different directions; Baker, Wife and
Little Red Ridinghood enter from another part of
the woods; music.*

BAKER: Are you certain this is the right direction?

LITTLE RED RIDINGHOOD: We went down the dell.

WIFE: Perhaps you forgot the way.

LITTLE RED RIDINGHOOD: The path is straight.

BAKER: Was straight. Now there is no path.

LITTLE RED RIDINGHOOD (*Increasingly upset*): Where's the stream?
Where's the lily pond? Where's Granny?

WIFE: Calm down.

The baby starts to cry.

(*To Baker*) Maybe we should turn back.

LITTLE RED RIDINGHOOD: NO!

BAKER: We will just have to find Granny's house without the
path.

LITTLE RED RIDINGHOOD (*Crying*): But Mother warned me never
to stray from the path!

BAKER: The path has strayed from you.

LITTLE RED RIDINGHOOD: Wait. That looks familiar. See, in the
distance, three oak trees.

We hear voices approaching.

BAKER: Yes. I recognize—

WIFE: Who might that be?

*Steward, Stepmother, Cinderella's Father, Lucinda
and Florinda, bedraggled, make their way downstage.*

BAKER: It's the steward and the royal family.

They bow.

What brings you into the woods?

CINDERELLA'S FATHER: The castle has been set upon by a giant.

WIFE: Oh, no . . .

BAKER (*To Steward*): I warned you! Why didn't you do something?

STEWARD: I don't make policy. I just carry it out!

Witch appears.

WITCH (*To Baker*): And I warned *you* that you can't count on a royal family to solve your problems.

WIFE: I think it best we go back to the village.

WITCH (*Bitter*): I wouldn't be in such a rush if I were you. Guess which path the giant took to the castle.

WIFE: Oh, no . . .

BAKER: What?

WITCH (*Displaying a small sack*): All that's left of my garden is a sack of beans—and there's not much left of your house either.

BAKER: But I heard giants never strike the same house twice.

WITCH: You heard wrong.

LITTLE RED RIDINGHOOD: Well, maybe we should go back to—

> *Suddenly the ground begins to shake. A frightening and increasingly loud crunching noise approaches. The huge shadow of a giant envelops the stage. The earth stops shaking as everyone looks up, astonished.*

WITCH (*Total amazement*): The giant's a woman!

BAKER: That size!

> *We do not see the giant, but when she speaks, the sound is loud and comes downward, from the direction of the shadow.*

GIANT: Where is the lad who killed my husband?

STEWARD: There is no lad here!

BAKER: We haven't seen him.

GIANT: I want the lad who climbed the beanstalk.

WITCH: We'll get him for you right away. Don't move!

> *Little Red Ridinghood pulls a knife from beneath her cape and runs towards the giant; Baker restrains her, but she threatens the giant anyway.*

LITTLE RED RIDINGHOOD: It was you who destroyed our house— not a great wind! It's because of you I've no mother!

GIANT: And who destroyed *my* house? That boy asked for shelter, and then he stole our gold, our hen, *and* our harp. Then he killed my husband. I must avenge the wrongdoings.

WIFE: We are not responsible for him.

WITCH: You're wasting your breath.

STEWARD: She's right. You can't reason with a dumb giant!

The ground gives a mighty shake; leaves and twigs fall from above.

GIANT: Not all giants are dumb. Give me the boy!

LITTLE RED RIDINGHOOD: We told you, he's not here!

CINDERELLA'S FATHER: The girl is telling the truth!

GIANT: I know he's there. And I'm going to wait right here until he's delivered to me.

Music.

NARRATOR: The giant, who was nearsighted, remained convinced that she had found the lad. There was no consensus among them as to which course of action to take.

WIFE: Put a spell on her.

WITCH: I no longer have my powers. If I did, you think I'd be standing here with all of you? (*Getting down to business*) Now, we'll have to give her someone.

OTHERS: Who?

WITCH: The steward. (*She grabs him and begins pulling him toward the giant*) It's in his line of duty to sacrifice his life—

STEWARD (*Struggling*): Don't be ridiculous! I'm not giving up my life for anyone!

He breaks loose; music stops.

GIANT: I'm waiting.

Music.

NARRATOR: You must understand, these were not people familiar with making choices—their past experiences in the woods had in no way prepared them to deal with a force *this* great.

WITCH (*Approaches the giant; confidential*): Excuse me. Would you like a blind girl, instead?

Florinda and Lucinda scream.

STEPMOTHER: How dare you!
WITCH: Put them out of their misery.
STEPSISTERS (*Bitter*): We're not *that* miserable!
BAKER: What are you talking about.
WIFE: She doesn't want a woman!
WITCH: Fine. Then what do *you* suggest we do?

Music stops.

GIANT: I'm still waiting.

Music.

NARRATOR: It is interesting to examine the moral issue at question here. The finality of stories such as these dictates—

Narrator turns upstage and notices everyone looking at him menacingly. They move towards him. Music stops.

(*To the group*) Sorry, I tell the story, I'm not part of it.

LITTLE RED RIDINGHOOD: That's right. (*Pulls out knife*)
WITCH: Not one of us.
BAKER: Always on the outside.

Baker grabs the Narrator and the group begins to pull him slowly towards the giant.

NARRATOR (*Nervous*): That's my role. You must understand, there must always be someone on the outside.
STEWARD: You're going to be on the inside now.
NARRATOR (*Frantic*): You're making a big mistake.
STEPMOTHER: Nonsense.
NARRATOR: You need an objective observer to pass the story along.
WITCH: Some of us don't like the way you've been telling it.

They pull him further.

NARRATOR: If you drag me into this mess, you'll never know how your story ends. You'll be lost!
BAKER (*To group*): Wait! He's the only one who knows the story.

They stop the struggle.

NARRATOR: Do you think it will be fun when you have to tell it yourselves? (*To Wife*) Think of your baby.

WIFE: Stop! He's right! Let him go!

Slowly and reluctantly, they let go of him.

(*To Little Red Ridinghood*) Put that knife away.

NARRATOR: Now, that's better. You don't want to live in a world of chaos. (*Calms down; begins to inch his way back to the apron*) There must always be an outside obser—

WITCH (*Screaming, racing towards the Narrator*): Here's the lad!

She grabs the Narrator and drags him across the stage and pushes him into the wing towards the giant; there is a sudden earth tremor; all eyes swoop upwards to suggest the Narrator has been picked up by the giant. We hear the Narrator yell from a distance.

NARRATOR (*Off*): I'm not the lad!

GIANT: This is not the lad.

BAKER: Don't drop—

Their eyes swing from the giant to the ground, and we hear a thud. They recoil in horror as we hear the Narrator splat; a beat.

BAKER (*To Witch*): Why did you push him into her arms?

WITCH (*Uneasy*): You wanted to get rid of him, too.

WIFE: We might have thought of something else.

WITCH: If it was up to you, a decision would never be made.

LITTLE RED RIDINGHOOD (*Looking towards Narrator's spot; panic*): Now that he's gone, we'll never know what will happen next.

WIFE: We'll manage.

GIANT: Must I search among you?!

Jack's Mother enters.

GROUP: No!

JACK'S MOTHER (*Tough*): Jack is just a boy! We had no food to eat and he sold his beloved cow in exchange for magic

103

beans. If anyone is to be punished, it's the man who made that exchange.

LITTLE RED RIDINGHOOD: That's right!

BAKER: Shhh.

WIFE (*Simultaneously*): Nonsense.

GIANT: He was your responsibility. Now I must punish him for his wrongs!

JACK'S MOTHER: We've suffered, too. Do you think it was a picnic disposing of your husband's remains?

GIANT: You are getting me angry!

JACK'S MOTHER (*More worked up*): What about *our* anger? What about *our* loss? Who has been flouncing through our kingdom?

STEWARD: Shhh. Be quiet.

JACK'S MOTHER (*More*): I'll hide my son and you'll never find him!

BAKER (*Through clenched teeth*): Don't upset the giant.

JACK'S MOTHER: You'll never, never find him!

GIANT: I'm warning you!

JACK'S MOTHER (*Out of control*): And if you don't go back this instant, we'll get *you* for all that *you've* done! We'll—

Steward comes behind her and slams her over the head with his staff. She staggers a moment, then stands motionless.

GIANT: Where is your son?

Rapunzel runs onstage screaming; she sees the giant.

Is that him?

Witch restrains Rapunzel.

WITCH (*To giant*): No. No. This is not the boy. (*To Rapunzel*) Stay here!

Rapunzel's Prince enters.

STEWARD (*To giant*): The boy is hiding in the steeple tower. You can find him there.

STEPMOTHER: Yes, that's true.

FLORINDA, LUCINDA: Yes . . .

RAPUNZEL'S PRINCE: Rapunzel! (*Signals to her*) Rapunzel!

GIANT: If he is not, I will return and find *you*!

> *We hear the giant beginning to depart. On the second footstep, Rapunzel runs toward the giant; Rapunzel's Prince races after her in panic.*

STEWARD (*To giant*): No! Don't step on the—

> *We hear a loud squishing noise; the group recoils in horror; after a stunned moment Rapunzel's Prince returns, shaking his head; Jack's Mother moans and Baker goes to her side. He touches her head and quickly pulls his hand back to discover it covered with blood.*

BAKER (*Panic-stricken*): She's in poor condition.

WIFE: Wake up.

JACK'S MOTHER (*Fighting for breath*): Don't let them get Jack.

WIFE: We won't.

JACK'S MOTHER: Promise me you won't let him be hurt. As I stand here at death's door.

BAKER: I'll do all I can.

JACK'S MOTHER (*Insistent*): Promise!

BAKER (*Annoyed*): All right. I promise!

> *Jack's Mother expires; Little Red Ridinghood sidles up to her and stares.*

WIFE: No, no. Come away from there. (*Pulls her away; to Steward*) You killed her!

STEWARD: I was thinking of the greater good. That's my job.

> *Music; Baker, Cinderella's Father and Steward drag Jack's Mother offstage. The group, hushed, watches; the Witch stands alone.*

WITCH (*Looking off after Rapunzel*):
> This is the world I meant.
> Couldn't you listen?
> Couldn't you stay content,
> Safe behind walls,
> As I
> Could not?
>   (*Looks at the group, then at us*)
> No matter what you say,

Children won't listen.
No matter what you know,
Children refuse
To learn.

Guide them along the way,
Still they won't listen.
Children can only grow
From something you love
To something you lose . . .

Steward and Cinderella's Father return, followed by Baker.

STEPMOTHER (*To Cinderella's Father*): Life was so steady, and now this! When are things going to return to normal?
STEWARD: We must be gone if we're to arrive before nightfall.
BAKER: Where are you going?
LUCINDA: We're off to a hidden kingdom.
STEPMOTHER: Shhh! We can't take everyone.
WITCH: Fools! There is nowhere to hide!

Music fades.

BAKER: You'll never get there. We have to stay here and find our way out of this together.
STEPMOTHER (*Sincere*): Some people are cut out to battle giants, and others are not. I don't have the constitution. And as long as I can be of no help, I'm going to hide. Everything will work out fine in the end.
BAKER: Not always.

Stepfamily and Steward exit.

LITTLE RED RIDINGHOOD: I hope the giant steps on them all.
WIFE: You shouldn't say that!

Witch, who has been quietly standing off to the side, turns around.

WITCH: You were thinking the same thing.
LITTLE RED RIDINGHOOD: This is terrible. We just saw three people die!
WITCH (*Bitter*): Since when are you so squeamish? How many wolves have *you* carved up?

LITTLE RED RIDINGHOOD: A wolf's not the same.

WITCH: Ask a wolf's mother!

BAKER: Stop it!

WITCH: I suggest we find that boy now and give her what she wants.

LITTLE RED RIDINGHOOD: If we give her the boy, she'll kill him, too.

WITCH: And if we don't, she'll kill half the kingdom!

WIFE: One step at a time. Maybe if he apologizes. Makes amends.

BAKER: Yes! He'll return the stolen goods.

LITTLE RED RIDINGHOOD: Yes!

WIFE: He's really a sweet boy at heart. She'll see that.

WITCH: You people are so blind. It's because of that boy there's a giant in our land. While you continue *talking* about this problem, *I'll* find that lad, and I'll serve him to the giant for lunch! (*She exits*)

LITTLE RED RIDINGHOOD: Are we going to let her feed the boy to the giant?

WIFE: No!

BAKER: I'll have to find him first.

WIFE: I'll go, too.

BAKER: No! Stay here with the baby.

WIFE: We'll fan out. It will increase our chances of finding him.

BAKER: What if one of us gets lost?

WIFE: We'll count our steps from right here.

Little Red Ridinghood comes over.

No. You stay here with the baby. I do not want you roaming about the woods.

BAKER: You would leave our child with her?

WIFE: Yes. The baby is asleep. He will be safe with the girl.

BAKER: But what if the giant were to return here—?

WIFE: The giant will not harm them. I know.

BAKER: How do you know?

WIFE: I know!

BAKER: But what if—

WIFE: But what if! BUT WHAT IF! Will only a giant's foot stop your arguing! One hundred paces—GO!

Music; pause.

BAKER: One . . . two . . . three . . . four . . .

The Baker and Wife march off in opposite directions, leaving Little Red Ridinghood and the baby; we follow the Wife as she crosses paths with Cinderella's Prince; she is nervous and excited in his presence; music fades.

WIFE: Eighty-one . . . eighty-two . . . eighty-three . . . eighty-four . . . (*She sees Prince and bows*) Hello, sir.

CINDERELLA'S PRINCE (*Continuing to walk*): Hello.

WIFE: You must be here to slay the giant.

CINDERELLA'S PRINCE: Yes.

WIFE: Have you come upon the giant yet?

CINDERELLA'S PRINCE: No.

WIFE: I have.

CINDERELLA'S PRINCE (*He stops*): You have?

WIFE: Yes.

CINDERELLA'S PRINCE: And why are you alone in the woods?

WIFE: I came with my husband. We were . . . well, it's a long story.

CINDERELLA'S PRINCE: He would let you roam alone in the woods?

WIFE: No, actually, it was my choice. I'm looking for a lad.

Music.

CINDERELLA'S PRINCE (*Moves closer*): Your choice? How brave.

WIFE: Brave?

CINDERELLA'S PRINCE (*Next to her*): Yes.

Anything can happen in the woods.
May I kiss you?

Wife blinks.

Any moment we could be crushed.

WIFE: Uh—

CINDERELLA'S PRINCE:

Don't feel rushed.

He kisses her. She is stunned, steps away and turns to us.

WIFE:
> This is ridiculous,
> What am I doing here?
> I'm in the wrong story.

She resumes the kiss, then pulls away; music stops.

> Wait one moment, please! We can't do this! You have a Princess.

CINDERELLA'S PRINCE: Well, yes, I do.
WIFE: And I have a . . . baker.
CINDERELLA'S PRINCE: Of course, you're right. How foolish.

Music resumes.

> Foolishness can happen in the woods.
> Once again, please—
> Let your hesitations be hushed.
> Any moment, big or small,
> Is a moment, after all.
> Seize the moment, skies may fall
> Any moment.

He kisses her again.

WIFE: But this is not right!
CINDERELLA'S PRINCE:
> Right and wrong don't matter in the woods,
> Only feelings.
> Let us meet the moment unblushed.
> Life is often so unpleasant—
> You must know that, as a peasant—
> Best to take the moment present
> As a present for the moment.

The Prince scoops up the Wife and carries her into a glade; elsewhere the Baker enters and encounters Cinderella at her Mother's grave; she is weeping.

BAKER (*Offstage, then entering*): Jack! Jack! Eighty-one . . . eighty-two . . . eighty-three . . .

He sees Cinderella; music fades.

What's wrong, ma'am? May I be of some service?

She turns away from him lest she be recognized.

CINDERELLA: The tree has fallen. Mother's grave, destroyed.
BAKER: Oh. I'm sorry.
CINDERELLA: My wishes have just been crushed.
BAKER: Don't say that.
CINDERELLA: It's true. You wouldn't understand.
BAKER: Well, you can't stay here. There's a giant on the loose.
CINDERELLA: I'm certain the Prince will see to it that the giant is rid from our land.
BAKER: There's been no sign of the Prince. No doubt he's off seducing some young maiden.
CINDERELLA (*Turning to him*): What?
BAKER: I understand that's what Princes do.
CINDERELLA (*Indignant*): Not every Prince!
BAKER: You look just like the Princess—but dirty.

    She turns away.

You *are* the Princess. (*He drops to his knees*)
CINDERELLA: Please. Get up. Get up! (*He does*) I'm not a Princess here.
BAKER: What are you to do?
CINDERELLA: I must be on my way back to the castle.
BAKER: You haven't heard? We came upon the royal family. The castle has been set upon by the giant.
CINDERELLA: And the Prince?
BAKER: He was not with them.

    Beat; music.

You must come with me. You shall be safe in our company.

    Reluctantly, she joins him and they exit; we return to Wife and Cinderella's Prince, who are on the ground, kissing; he pulls away; music stops.

CINDERELLA'S PRINCE: I must leave you.
WIFE (*Flustered*): Why?
CINDERELLA'S PRINCE: The giant.

    Music.

WIFE: The giant. I had almost forgotten. Will we find each
    other in the woods again?
CINDERELLA'S PRINCE:

This was just a moment in the woods.
Our moment,
Shimmering and lovely and sad.
Leave the moment, just be glad
For the moment that we had.
Every moment is of moment
When you're in the woods . . .

Music continues under.

(*Smooth*) Now I must go off to slay a giant. That is
what the *next* moment holds for me. (*He gives her a
quick kiss*) I shall not forget you. How brave you are to
be alone in the woods. And how alive you've made
me feel. (*He exits*)

Wife sits, stunned; music stops.

WIFE: What was that?

Music resumes.

Was that me?
Was that him?
Did a Prince really kiss me?
And kiss me?
And kiss me?
And did I kiss him back?

Was it wrong?
Am I mad?
Is that all?
Does he miss me?
Was he suddenly
Getting bored with me?
   (*She stands*)
Wake up! Stop dreaming.
Stop prancing about the woods.
It's not beseeming.
What is it about the woods?
   (*Firm*)

111

INTO THE WOODS

Back to life, back to sense,
Back to child, back to husband,
No one lives in the woods.
There are vows, there are ties,
There are needs, there are standards,
There are shouldn'ts and shoulds.

Why not both instead?
There's the answer, if you're clever:
Have a child for warmth,
And a baker for bread,
And a Prince for whatever—

Never!
It's these woods.

Face the facts, find the boy,
Join the group, stop the giant—
Just get out of these woods.
Was that him? Yes, it was.
Was that me? No, it wasn't,
Just a trick of the woods.

Just a moment,
One peculiar passing moment.

Must it all be either less or more,
Either plain or grand?
Is it always "or"?
Is it never "and"?
That's what woods are for:
For those moments in the woods . . .

Oh, if life were made of moments,
Even now and then a bad one—!
But if life were only moments,
Then you'd never know you had one.

First a witch, then a child,
Then a Prince, then a moment—
Who can live in the woods?
And to get what you wish,
Only just for a moment—
These are dangerous woods . . .

Let the moment go . . .
Don't forget it for a moment, though.
Just remembering you've had an "and,"
When you're back to "or,"
Makes the "or" mean more
Than it did before.
Now I understand—
    (*Sighs, starts walking faster*)
And it's time to leave the woods.

Wife begins counting her steps as she heads off-stage. She stops and retraces her steps, uncertain of her direction. She begins to go in another direction when she stops, hearing the approach of the giant in the distance. The sound moves steadily towards her. In panic she retreats. Loud noise and dramatic light and set change as Wife falls backwards. Blackout. Music fades. Lights up on Baker, Cinderella and Little Red Ridinghood.

BAKER (*Worried*): She should be back by now.
LITTLE RED RIDINGHOOD: She wouldn't get lost.
CINDERELLA: I'm sure she'll return.
BAKER: No. I must go in search of her.
LITTLE RED RIDINGHOOD: We'll come, too.
BAKER: No. You stay here. I will count one hundred paces. I shall return soon.

Witch makes a noisy entrance with Jack in tow; she keeps a firm grip on his ear. Jack drops Wife's scarf as he enters.

WITCH: Look who I found!
JACK: Please don't let her give me to the giant!
WITCH: It's not our fault the giant wants you!
JACK: You're hurting me.

Baker notices scarf, goes over and picks it up.

CINDERELLA: Let go of him!
LITTLE RED RIDINGHOOD: Leave him alone!
BAKER (*Quiet*): Where did you find this?

Witch lets go of Jack, who runs behind Baker for protection.

Where is my wife?

Beat.

WITCH: She's dead.

BAKER (*Stunned*): What?

JACK: I'm sorry, sir. I came upon her. She was under a tree . . .

WITCH: He was sobbing over her like she was his own mother.

CINDERELLA: How awful . . .

BAKER (*Beat; lost*): How could this happen? I should never have let her wander off *alone*.

JACK: I buried her in a footprint.

BAKER: I should have insisted she stay home.

WITCH (*Impatient*): Remorse will get you nowhere.

BAKER (*Angry*): My wife is dead!

WITCH: Wake up! People are dying all around you. You're not the only one to suffer a loss. When you're dead, you're dead. (*Advancing towards Jack*) Now it's time to get this boy to the giant before we're all so much dead meat. Boom crunch!

She goes toward Jack; music.

CINDERELLA (*Protecting Jack*): Keep away from him!

LITTLE RED RIDINGHOOD (*Joining Cinderella*): No!

WITCH: This is no time to be soft-hearted! He's going to the giant and I'm taking him—

BAKER (*Advancing, distraught*): Yes! He's the one to blame! (*To Jack*) It's because of you there's a giant in our midst and my wife is dead!

JACK:

But it isn't my fault,
I was given those beans!
(*To Baker*)
You persuaded me to trade away
My cow for beans!
And without those beans
There'd have been no stalk
To get up to the giants
In the first place!

BAKER:

>Wait a minute, *magic* beans
>For a cow so old
>That you had to tell
>A lie to sell
>It, which you told!
>Were they worthless beans?
>Were they oversold?
>Oh, and tell us who
>Persuaded you
>To steal that gold!

LITTLE RED RIDINGHOOD (*To Jack*):

>See, it's your fault.

JACK:

>No!

BAKER:

>So it's your fault . . .

JACK:

>No!

LITTLE RED RIDINGHOOD:

>Yes, it is!

JACK:

>It's not!

BAKER:

>It's true.

JACK:

>Wait a minute, though—
>I only stole the gold
>To get my cow back
>From you!

LITTLE RED RIDINGHOOD (*To Baker*):

>So it's your fault!

JACK:

>Yes!

BAKER:

>No, it isn't!
>I'd have kept those beans,

But our house was cursed.
(*Referring to Witch*)
She made us get a cow to get
The curse reversed!

WITCH:

It's his father's fault
That the curse got placed
And the place got cursed
In the first place!

LITTLE RED RIDINGHOOD:
Oh.
Then it's his fault!

WITCH:
So.

CINDERELLA:
It was his fault . . .

JACK:
No.

BAKER:
Yes, it is,
It's his.

CINDERELLA:
I guess . . .

JACK:
Wait a minute, though—
I chopped down the beanstalk,
Right? That's clear.
But without any beanstalk,
Then what's queer
Is how did the second giant get down here
In the first place?
(*Confused*)
Second place . . .

CINDERELLA:
Yes!

LITTLE RED RIDINGHOOD:
How?

BAKER:
> Hmm . . .

JACK:
> Well,
> Who had the other bean?

BAKER:
> The other bean?

CINDERELLA:
> The other bean?

JACK (*To Baker*):
> You pocketed the other bean.

BAKER:
> I didn't!
> Yes, I did.

LITTLE RED RIDINGHOOD:
> So it's *your* f—!

BAKER:
> No, it isn't,
> 'Cause I gave it to my wife!

LITTLE RED RIDINGHOOD:
> So it's *her* f—!

BAKER:
> *No, it isn't!*

CINDERELLA:
> Then whose is it?

BAKER:
> Wait a minute!
> (*To Cinderella*)
> She exchanged that bean
> To obtain your shoe,
> So the one who knows what happened
> To the bean is *you*!

CINDERELLA:
> You mean *that* old bean—
> That your *wife*—? Oh, dear—

(*As they all look at her*)
But I never knew,
And so I threw—
Well, don't look here!

LITTLE RED RIDINGHOOD:
So it's your fault!

CINDERELLA:
But—

JACK:
See, it's her fault—

CINDERELLA:
But—

JACK:
And it isn't mine at all!

BAKER (*To Cinderella*):
But what?

CINDERELLA (*To Jack*):
Well, if you hadn't gone
Back up again—

JACK:
We were needy—

CINDERELLA:
You were greedy!
Did you need that hen?

JACK:
But I got it for my mother—!

LITTLE RED RIDINGHOOD:
So it's *her* fault then!

CINDERELLA:
Yes, and what about the harp
In the third place?

BAKER:
The harp—yes!

JACK (*Referring to Little Red Ridinghood*):
She went and dared me to!

LITTLE RED RIDINGHOOD:
> *I* dared you to?

JACK:
> You dared me to!
> (*To the others*)
> She said that I was scared—

LITTLE RED RIDINGHOOD:
> *Me?*

JACK:
> —to.
> She dared me!

LITTLE RED RIDINGHOOD:
> No, I didn't!

BAKER, CINDERELLA, JACK:
> So it's your fault!

LITTLE RED RIDINGHOOD:
> Wait a minute—!

CINDERELLA:
> If you hadn't dared him to—

BAKER (*To Jack*):
> And you had left the harp alone,
> We wouldn't be in trouble
> In the first place!

LITTLE RED RIDINGHOOD (*To Cinderella, overlapping*):
> Well, if you hadn't thrown away the bean
> In the first place—!
> It was your fault!

CINDERELLA (*Looking at Witch*):
> Well, if she hadn't raised them in the first place—!

JACK (*Overlapping, to Witch*):
> Yes, if you hadn't raised them in the first place—!

LITTLE RED RIDINGHOOD, BAKER (*To Witch*):
> Right! It's you who raised them in the first place—!

CINDERELLA (*Simultaneously*):
> You raised the beans in the first place!

JACK:
> It's *your* fault!

CINDERELLA, JACK, LITTLE RED RIDINGHOOD, BAKER:
> You're responsible!
> You're the one to blame!
> It's your fault!

WITCH:
> Shhhhhhhhhhh!

> *They stop in their tracks; beat.*

> It's the last midnight.
> It's the last wish.
> It's the last midnight,
> Soon it will be boom—

> *Stamps her foot; drum.*

> Squish!

> *Squishes.*

> Told a little lie,
> Stole a little gold,
> Broke a little vow,
> Did you?
> Had to get your Prince,
> Had to get your cow,
> Have to get your wish,
> Doesn't matter how—
> Anyway, it doesn't matter now.

> It's the last midnight,
> It's the boom—
> Splat!
> Nothing but a vast midnight,
> Everybody smashed flat!

> Nothing we can do . . .
> Not exactly true:
> We can always give her the boy . . .

> *They protect Jack as she reaches for him.*

> No?

No, of course what really matters
Is the blame,
Someone you can blame.
Fine, if that's the thing you enjoy,
Placing the blame,
If that's the aim,
Give me the blame—
Just give me the boy.

LITTLE RED RIDINGHOOD, CINDERELLA: No!
WITCH (*To all*):
    No . . .
    You're so nice.
    You're not good,
    You're not bad,
    You're just nice.
    I'm not good,
    I'm not nice,
    I'm just right.
    I'm the witch.
    You're the world.

    I'm the hitch,
    I'm what no one believes,
    I'm the witch.
    You're all liars and thieves,
    Like his father,
    Like his son will be, too—
    Oh, why bother?
    You'll just do what you do.

    It's the last midnight,
    So goodbye, all.
    Coming at you fast, midnight—
    Soon you'll see the sky fall.

    Here, you want a bean?

She starts scattering her beans all around; the others frantically try to pick them all up.

    Have another bean.
    Beans were made for making you rich!
    Plant them and they soar—

Here, you want some more?
Listen to the roar:
Giants by the score—!
Oh well, you can blame another witch.

It's the last midnight,
It's the last verse.
Now, before it's past midnight,
I'm leaving you my last curse:

I'm leaving you alone.
You can tend the garden, it's yours.
Separate and alone,
Everybody down on all fours.

(*Looking upward*)
All right, Mother, when?
Lost the beans again!
Punish me the way you did then!
Give me claws and a hunch,
Just away from this bunch
And the gloom
And the doom
And the boom
Cruuunch!

She disappears; long beat. Everybody slowly rises.

JACK (*Quiet*): Maybe I shouldn't have stolen from the giant . . .

LITTLE RED RIDINGHOOD (*Quiet*): Maybe I shouldn't have strayed from the path . . .

CINDERELLA (*Quiet*): Maybe I shouldn't have attended the Ball . . .

BAKER (*Bitter*): Yes. Maybe you shouldn't have . . . (*He begins to exit*)

JACK: Where are you going?

BAKER: Away from here.

LITTLE RED RIDINGHOOD (*Frightened*): But you said we had to find our way out of this together.

BAKER: It doesn't matter whether we're together or apart.

JACK: We need your help.

BAKER: You don't understand. My wife was the one who really helped. I depended on her for everything. (*Moves further away*)

CINDERELLA: You would leave your child?

BAKER (*Despondent*): My child will be happier in the arms of a
    Princess . . . (*He exits*)

CINDERELLA: But wait . . .

> *Music; another part of the woods. Baker crosses*
> *stage and is startled by Mysterious Man.*

BAKER: I thought you were dead.

MYSTERIOUS MAN (*Bright*): Not completely. Are we ever?

BAKER (*Cold*): As far as I'm concerned, you are.

MYSTERIOUS MAN: Is that true?

BAKER: It's because of you all of this happened.

MYSTERIOUS MAN: I strayed into the garden to give your mother
    a gift. And I foolishly took some of those beans for
    myself. How was I to know? How are we ever to
    know? And when she died, I ran from my guilt. And
    now, aren't you making the same mistake?

BAKER: No. (*He begins to exit*)

MYSTERIOUS MAN: Aren't you running away?

BAKER:
> No more questions.
> Please.
> No more tests.
> Comes the day you say, "What for?"
> Please—no more.

MYSTERIOUS MAN:
> We disappoint,
> We disappear,
> We die but we don't . . .

BAKER: What?

MYSTERIOUS MAN:
> They disappoint
> In turn, I fear.
> Forgive, though, they won't . . .

BAKER:
> No more riddles.
> No more jests.
> No more curses you can't undo,
> Left by fathers you never knew.

No more quests.
No more feelings.
Time to shut the door.
Just—no more.
  (*He sits in despair*)

MYSTERIOUS MAN:

Running away—let's do it,
Free from the ties that bind.
No more despair
Or burdens to bear
Out there in the yonder.

Running away—go to it.
Where did you have in mind?
Have to take care:
Unless there's a "where,"
You'll only be wandering blind.
Just more questions,
Different kind.

Where are we to go?
Where are we ever to go?

Running away—we'll do it.
Why sit around, resigned?
Trouble is, son,
The farther you run,
The more you feel undefined
For what you have left undone
And, more, what you've left behind.

We disappoint,
We leave a mess,
We die but we don't . . .

BAKER:

We disappoint
In turn, I guess.
Forget, though, we won't . . .

BOTH:

Like father, like son.

Mysterious Man disappears.

124

BAKER:

> No more giants,
> Waging war.
> Can't we just pursue our lives
> With our children and our wives?
> Till that happier day arrives,
> How do you ignore
> All the witches,
> All the curses,
> All the wolves, all the lies,
> The false hopes, the goodbyes, the reverses,
> All the wondering what even worse is
> Still in store?
>
> All the children . . .
> All the giants . . .
> *(After a moment's thought)*
> No more.

With resolve, Baker returns to the waiting group.

CINDERELLA: I knew you wouldn't give up.

JACK: He wouldn't leave his baby.

LITTLE RED RIDINGHOOD: It looked like he was going to.

Cinderella and Jack shoot her a look.

BAKER: Give me my son.

He takes baby in his arms; baby begins to cry.

He always cries when I—

He pulls baby close to him and baby stops crying; beat.

CINDERELLA: Now what are we to do?

BAKER: We must have a plan before the giant returns.

JACK: What?

BAKER: We all have to think!

JACK: If there were just some way we could surprise her.

LITTLE RED RIDINGHOOD: She's too tall to surprise.

Birds descend.

CINDERELLA: Oh, good friends. I need your help now more than ever.

She listens.

What of the Prince?

She listens with resolve.

I don't care! What's important now is that we find a way to fell the giant. How can you help?

She listens.

You could do that?

She listens.

How can I ever thank you?

Birds fly off.

LITTLE RED RIDINGHOOD: You can talk to birds?
CINDERELLA: The birds will help.
JACK: How?
CINDERELLA: When the giant returns, they'll attack her and peck out her eyes till she's blind.
BAKER: What good will that do?
CINDERELLA: Then you can surprise her. Strike her, or whatever you do to kill a giant.
BAKER: Once she's blinded, she'll stagger about.
JACK: She'll get angry.
LITTLE RED RIDINGHOOD: And she'll crush us all.

Beat.

BAKER: Smear the ground with pitch.
CINDERELLA: Yes!
BAKER: We'll lure her to an area smeared with pitch.
CINDERELLA: Her shoes will stick, and she won't be able to move.
JACK: And I will climb a tree and strike her from behind.
BAKER: I will climb the tree, too. It may take two mighty blows.
LITTLE RED RIDINGHOOD: I'm excited!
JACK: I'm going to kill another giant!
BAKER: Quick! It will be dark soon. We must find the pitch.

They begin to exit; Baker stops and hands the baby to Cinderella.

The baby will be safest here with you. This will take no time.

Baker, Little Red Ridinghood and Jack exit. Baby begins to cry.

CINDERELLA: Oh, no. Now, now. Don't cry, little one. I know. You want your mother.

Baby begins to calm down; Cinderella's Prince bounds onstage; he doesn't recognize Cinderella.

CINDERELLA'S PRINCE: Hello. (*He begins to cross the stage*)
CINDERELLA: The giant went in that direction.
CINDERELLA'S PRINCE (*Realizing it is Cinderella*): My darling. I did not recognize you. What are you doing in those old clothes? And with a child? You must go back to the castle at once. There's a giant on the loose.
CINDERELLA: The giant has been to the castle.
CINDERELLA'S PRINCE: No! Are you all right?

He moves to her; she nods and walks away.

My love. Why are you being so cold?
CINDERELLA: Maybe because I'm not your only love. Am I?
CINDERELLA'S PRINCE (*Beat*): I love you. Truly I do. (*Pause*) But yes, it's true.
CINDERELLA: Why, if you love me, would you have strayed?
CINDERELLA'S PRINCE: I thought if you were mine, that I would never wish for more. And part of me is content and as happy as I've ever been. But there remains a part of me that continually needs more.
CINDERELLA: I have, on occasion, wanted more. But that doesn't mean I went in search of it. If this is how you behave as a Prince, what kind of King will you be?
CINDERELLA'S PRINCE: I was raised to be charming, not sincere. I didn't ask to be born a King, and I am not perfect. I am only human.
CINDERELLA: I think you should go.
CINDERELLA'S PRINCE: Leave? But I *do* love you.
CINDERELLA: Consider that I have been lost. A victim of the giant.
CINDERELLA'S PRINCE: Is that what you really wish?

CINDERELLA: My father's house was a nightmare. Your house was a dream. Now I want something in-between. Please go.

He begins to exit.

CINDERELLA'S PRINCE: I shall always love the maiden who ran away.

CINDERELLA: And I the faraway Prince.

He exits. Another moment for Cinderella with the baby. Little Red Ridinghood enters.

LITTLE RED RIDINGHOOD: They're almost finished. You see over there between those two trees? When the giant comes, we are to send her over there.

CINDERELLA: Good.

LITTLE RED RIDINGHOOD: I wanted to climb the tree, too.

CINDERELLA: I'm glad you're here to help me.

Little Red Ridinghood begins to cry; music.

What's wrong?

LITTLE RED RIDINGHOOD: My granny's gone.

CINDERELLA (*Moves to comfort her*): Oh, no. I'm so sorry.

LITTLE RED RIDINGHOOD: I think my granny and my mother would be upset with me.

CINDERELLA: Why?

LITTLE RED RIDINGHOOD: They said to always make them proud. And here I am about to kill somebody.

CINDERELLA: Not somebody. A giant who has been doing harm.

LITTLE RED RIDINGHOOD: But the giant's a person. Aren't we to show forgiveness? Mother would be very unhappy with these circumstances.

CINDERELLA:
Mother cannot guide you.
Now you're on your own.
Only me beside you.
Still, you're not alone.
No one is alone, truly.
No one is alone.

Sometimes people leave you,
Halfway through the wood.

Others may deceive you.
You decide what's good.
You decide alone.
But no one is alone.

LITTLE RED RIDINGHOOD:
I wish . . .

CINDERELLA:
I know . . .

Little Red Ridinghood moves close to Cinderella, who comforts her; Jack and the Baker, atop nearby trees.

JACK: Wait until my mother hears I've slain the giant.

BAKER: Jack. Your mother is dead.

JACK (*Stunned*): Dead? Was she killed by the giant?

BAKER: She was arguing with the giant—trying to protect you—and she was struck a deadly blow by the Prince's steward.

JACK: Oh no. Why would he do that?

BAKER: He was afraid she was provoking the giant.

JACK (*Upset*): Can no one bring her back?

BAKER: No one.

JACK: The steward will pay for this. After we slay the giant, I will slay him.

BAKER: You'll do nothing of the kind!

JACK: But he shouldn't have killed my mother. Right?

BAKER: I guess not.

JACK (*Cold*): Then he must die.

BAKER: Well, no.

JACK (*Getting worked up*): Why not?

BAKER: Because that would be wrong.

JACK: What he did was wrong. He should be punished.

BAKER: He will be, somehow.

JACK: How?

BAKER: I don't know! (*Angry*) Stop asking me questions I can't answer.

JACK (*Cold*): I'm going to kill him!

BAKER: Then kill him! (*Beat*) No, don't kill him.

Music.

CINDERELLA (*To Little Red Ridinghood*):
>   Mother isn't here now.

BAKER (*To Jack*):
>   Wrong things, right things . . .

CINDERELLA:
>   Who knows what she'd say?

BAKER:
>   Who can say what's true?

CINDERELLA:
>   Nothing's quite so clear now—

BAKER:
>   Do things, fight things . . .

CINDERELLA:
>   Feel you've lost your way?

BAKER:
>   You decide,
>   But you are not alone.

CINDERELLA (*Overlapping*):
>   You are not alone,
>   Believe me.
>   No one is alone.

BAKER:
>   No one is alone,
>   Believe me.

CINDERELLA:
>   Truly . . .

BAKER, CINDERELLA:
>   You move just a finger,
>   Say the slightest word,
>   Something's bound to linger,
>   Be heard.

BAKER:
>   No one acts alone.
>   Careful,
>   No one is alone.

BAKER, CINDERELLA:
>People make mistakes.

BAKER:
>Fathers,

CINDERELLA:
>Mothers,

BAKER, CINDERELLA:
>People make mistakes,
>Holding to their own,
>Thinking they're alone.

CINDERELLA:
>Honor their mistakes—

BAKER:
>Fight for their mistakes—

CINDERELLA:
>Everybody makes—

BAKER, CINDERELLA:
>—one another's
>Terrible mistakes.
>Witches can be right,
>Giants can be good.
>You decide what's right,
>You decide what's good.

CINDERELLA:
>Just remember:

BAKER:
>Just remember:

BAKER, CINDERELLA:
>Someone is on your side.

JACK, LITTLE RED RIDINGHOOD:
>*Our* side.

BAKER, CINDERELLA:
>Our side—
>Someone else is not.
>While we're seeing our side—

JACK, LITTLE RED RIDINGHOOD:
>Our side . . .

BAKER, CINDERELLA:
>Our side—

BAKER, CINDERELLA, LITTLE RED RIDINGHOOD, JACK:
>Maybe we forgot:
>They are not alone.
>No one is alone.

CINDERELLA:
>Hard to see the light now.

BAKER:
>Just don't let it go.

BAKER, CINDERELLA:
>Things will come out right now.
>We can make it so.
>Someone is on your side—

>*Song is interrupted by the sound of the giant approaching in the distance; music fades.*

LITTLE RED RIDINGHOOD: Here she comes.
CINDERELLA: Remember. Don't let her know our plan.

>*Ground trembles; shadow is cast.*

GIANT: Where is the boy?
LITTLE RED RIDINGHOOD (*Yelling upwards*): We don't know!
CINDERELLA: Yes we do! We can't go on hiding him any longer. He must pay the price for his wrongs.
GIANT: Quick! Tell me where he is.
LITTLE RED RIDINGHOOD (*Points*): Over there.
CINDERELLA: See that tree where the birds are clustered? Jack is in that tree, hiding.
GIANT: Thank you. Now justice will be served and I shall leave your kingdom.

>*Giant turns and heads away. We hear the sounds of birds attacking in the distance; Cinderella and Little Red Ridinghood watch eagerly. We barely hear them over the roar of the giant; music.*

CINDERELLA: Good birds!

Cry from the giant.

LITTLE RED RIDINGHOOD: She doesn't look happy.

We hear the giant pounded on the head; another cry.

CINDERELLA (*Grimace*): Ouch!

Another cry.

LITTLE RED RIDINGHOOD (*Disgusted*): The club is stuck in her head!

CINDERELLA: They've done it! She's swaying.

LITTLE RED RIDINGHOOD: She's bleeding all over.

CINDERELLA: She's beginning to fall!

LITTLE RED RIDINGHOOD (*Panicked*): She's beginning to fall this way!

They back off the stage quickly, as the loudest noise of all resounds. The giant's forehead and mane of hair fall from the wing. Little Red Ridinghood and Cinderella race off in the direction of Jack and the Baker. Finale music begins. During the following sequence the characters enter, give their morals and remain onstage.

JACK'S MOTHER:
The slotted spoon *can* catch the potato . . .

MYSTERIOUS MAN:
Every knot was once straight rope . . .

Princes enter with Snow White and Sleeping Beauty.

PRINCES:
The harder to wake, the better to have . . .

SNOW WHITE, SLEEPING BEAUTY (*Yawn*):
Excuse me.

STEWARD:
The greater the good, the harder the blow . . .

STEPMOTHER:
> When going to hide, know how to get there.

CINDERELLA'S FATHER:
> And how to get back . . .

FLORINDA, LUCINDA:
> And eat first . . .

GRANNY:
> The knife that is sharp today may be dull by to-
> morrow . . .

RAPUNZEL:
> Ah-ah-ah-ah-ah . . .

> *Jack, Baker, Cinderella and Little Red Ridinghood
> enter from upstage of giant's head. Music con-
> tinues under.*

BAKER: Now we can all return home and let us hope there will
> be no more killing.
JACK: Where am I to go? I have no one to take care of me.
BAKER: You'll have to take care of yourself now, Jack. It's time.
LITTLE RED RIDINGHOOD: No it's not. I'll take care of him.
JACK: You will?
LITTLE RED RIDINGHOOD: Yes. I'll be your mother now.
JACK: I don't want another mother, I want a friend. And a pet.
LITTLE RED RIDINGHOOD (*To Baker*): Of course, we have nowhere
> to go, so we'll move in with you.
BAKER: Oh, no.
LITTLE RED RIDINGHOOD: It'll be fun!
BAKER: My house is a shambles and there is hardly room for—
LITTLE RED RIDINGHOOD: It'll be fun!
BAKER: No. You don't— (*Beat*) Of course you can come home
> with us.
JACK (*To Cinderella*): And you shall join us, too.
BAKER: You'll not return to the castle?
CINDERELLA: I'll gladly help you with your house. There are
> times when I actually enjoy cleaning.

> *Beat.*

BAKER (*Stepping away*): How proud my wife would have been of us. And how sad it is that my son will never know her.

Baby cries.

Maybe I just wasn't meant to have children—

WIFE (*Enters behind him*):
　　Don't say that!
　　Of course you were meant to have children . . .

BAKER:

　　But how will I go about being a father
　　With no one to mother my child?

Baby cries.

WIFE:

　　Just calm the child.

BAKER (*Attempting to do so*):
　　Yes, calm the child.

WIFE:

　　Look, tell him the story
　　Of how it all happened.
　　Be father and mother,
　　You'll know what to do.

BAKER:

　　Alone . . .

WIFE:

　　Sometimes people leave you
　　Halfway through the wood.
　　Do not let it grieve you,
　　No one leaves for good.
　　You are not alone.
　　No one is alone.

　　Hold him to the light now,
　　Let him see the glow.
　　Things will be all right now.

Baby whimpers.

Tell him what you know . . .

Baby cries.

BAKER: Shhh. Once upon a time . . .

Witch enters.

. . . in a far-off kingdom . . . lived a young maiden,
. . . a sad young lad . . . and a childless baker . . .
with his wife.

WITCH (*Simultaneously with Baker*):
Careful the things you say,
Children will listen.
Careful the things you do,
Children will see.
And learn.

Children may not obey,
But children will listen.
Children will look to you
For which way to turn,
To learn what to be.

Careful before you say,
"Listen to me."
Children will listen.

COMPANY:
Careful the wish you make,
Wishes are children.
Careful the path they take—
Wishes come true,
Not free.

Careful the spell you cast,
Not just on children.
Sometimes the spell may last
Past what you can see
And turn against you . . .

WITCH:
Careful the tale you tell.
That is the spell.
Children will listen . . .

COMPANY (*In three groups*):
>Though it's fearful,
>Though it's deep, though it's dark
>And though you may lose the path,
>Though you may encounter wolves,
>You can't just act,
>You have to listen.
>You can't just act,
>You have to think.
>
>Though it's dark,
>There are always wolves,
>There are always spells,
>There are always beans,
>Or a giant dwells there.
>
>   (*In unison*)
>So
>Into the woods you go again,
>You have to every now and then.
>Into the woods, no telling when,
>Be ready for the journey.
>
>Into the woods, but not too fast
>Or what you wish you lose at last.
>Into the woods, but mind the past.
>Into the woods, but mind the future.
>Into the woods, but not to stray,
>Or tempt the wolf or steal from the giant—
>
>The way is dark,
>The light is dim,
>But now there's you,
>Me, her and him.
>The chances look small,
>The choices look grim,
>But everything you learn there
>Will help when you return there.

BAKER, JACK, CINDERELLA, LITTLE RED RIDINGHOOD (*Softly*):
>The light is getting dimmer . . .

BAKER:
>I think I see a glimmer—

INTO THE WOODS

ALL:

Into the woods—you have to grope,
But that's the way you learn to cope.
Into the woods to find there's hope
Of getting through the journey.

Into the woods, each time you go,
There's more to learn of what you know.
Into the woods, but not too slow—
Into the woods, it's nearing midnight—

Into the woods
To mind the wolf,
To heed the witch,
To honor the giant,
To mind,
To heed,
To find,
To think,
To teach,
To join,
To go to the Festival!

Into the woods,
Into the woods,
Into the woods,
Then out of the woods—
And happy ever after!

CINDERELLA:

I wish . . .

Pause; chord; blackout.

THE END

STEPHEN SONDHEIM wrote the music and lyrics for *Saturday Night* (1954), *A Funny Thing Happened on the Way to the Forum* (1962), *Anyone Can Whistle* (1964), *Company* (1970), *Follies* (1971), *A Little Night Music* (1973), *The Frogs* (1974), *Pacific Overtures* (1976), *Sweeney Todd* (1979), *Merrily We Roll Along* (1981), *Sunday in the Park with George* (1984), *Into the Woods* (1987), *Assassins* (1991), *Passion* (1994) and *Road Show* (2008), as well as the lyrics for *West Side Story* (1957), *Gypsy* (1959), *Do I Hear a Waltz?* (1965), and additional lyrics for *Candide* (1973). *Side by Side by Sondheim* (1976), *Marry Me a Little* (1981), *You're Gonna Love Tomorrow* (1983), *Putting It Together* (1993, 1999), *Moving On* (2001) and *Sondheim on Sondheim* (2010) are anthologies of his work as composer and lyricist.

For film, he composed the scores of *Stavisky* (1974), co-composed the score for *Reds* (1981) and wrote songs for *Dick Tracy* (1990). He wrote songs for the television production *Evening Primrose* (1966), co-authored the film *The Last of Sheila* (1973) and the play *Getting Away with Murder* (1996), and provided incidental music for the plays *The Girls of Summer* (1956), *Invitation to a March* (1961), *Twigs* (1971) and *The Enclave* (1973).

Mr. Sondheim has received the Tony Award for Best Score/Music/ Lyrics for *Company*, *Follies*, *A Little Night Music*, *Into the Woods*, *Sweeney Todd* and *Passion*, all of which won the New York Drama Critics Circle Award for Outstanding/Best Musical, as did *Pacific Overtures* and *Sunday in the Park with George*

In total, his works have accumulated more than sixty individual and collaborative Tony Awards. "Sooner or Later" from the film *Dick Tracy* won the 1990 Academy Award for Best Song. Mr. Sondheim received the Pulitzer Prize for Drama in 1984 for *Sunday in the Park with George*. In 1983 he was elected to the American Academy of Arts and Letters, which awarded him the Gold Medal for Music in 2006. In 1990 he was appointed the first Visiting Professor of Contemporary Theatre at Oxford University. In 1993 he received the Kennedy Center Honors Lifetime Achievement Award.

Mr. Sondheim is on the Council of the Dramatists Guild, the national association of playwrights, composers and lyricists, having served as its president from 1973 to 1981. In 1981 he founded Young Playwrights Inc. to develop and promote the work of American playwrights ages eighteen years and younger. His collected lyrics with attendant essays have been published in two volumes: *Finishing the Hat* (2010) and *Look, I Made a Hat* (2011). In 2010 the Broadway theater formerly known as Henry Miller's Theatre was renamed in his honor.

JAMES LAPINE has worked with Stephen Sondheim on *Sunday in the Park with George, Into the Woods* and *Passion*. He also directed *Merrily We Roll Along* for Encores, and the original revue *Sondheim on Sondheim* for the Roundabout Theatre Company.

With William Finn, he has worked on *Falsettos, A New Brain, The 25th Annual Putnam County Spelling Bee* and *Little Miss Sunshine*.

He has written six plays: *Table Settings; Twelve Dreams; Luck, Pluck & Virtue; The Moment When; Fran's Bed* and *Mrs. Miller Does Her Thing*. He adapted Moss Hart's memoir *Act One* for Lincoln Center Theater.

He has received twelve Tony nominations, winning three times, and he has been awarded five Drama Desk Awards. In 1984 he was awarded the Pulitzer Prize for Drama for *Sunday in the Park with George*. Additional Broadway directing credits include *The Diary of Anne Frank, Golden Child, Annie, Amour* and *Dirty Blonde*.

He directed the films *Impromptu, Life with Mikey* and *Earthly Possessions*, and he wrote the screenplay for the film version of *Into the Woods*. He received the Peabody Award for his documentary *Six by Sondheim*, which aired on HBO, and for which he received an Emmy Award nomination.